THE MORAVIANS

IN

NORTH CAROLINA.

AN AUTHENTIC HISTORY.

BY

Rev. LEVIN T. REICHEL,
OF SALEM, N. C.

Notice

In many older books, foxing (or discoloration) occurs and, in some instances, print lightens with wear and age. Reprinted books, such as this, often duplicate these flaws, notwithstanding efforts to reduce or eliminate them. The pages of this reprint have been digitally enhanced and, where possible, the flaws eliminated in order to provide clarity of content and a pleasant reading experience.

Copyright © 1857, Levin T. Reichel

Originally Published:
Philadelphia:
1857

Reprinted by:

Janaway Publishing, Inc.
732 Kelsey Ct.
Santa Maria, California 93454
(805) 925-1038
www.janawaygenealogy.com

2012

ISBN: 978-1-59641-272-9

Seal on the Cover:
Moravian Seal, or Agnus Dei, stained glass window in the Rights Chapel at Trinity Moravian Church, Winston-Salem, North Carolina

Made in the United States of America

CONTENTS.

		PAGE
1. North Carolina in 1752	. . . .	13
2. Wachovia	. . . . . .	22
3. First Settlement at Bethabara, 1753	. .	28
4. Indian War. Bethania, 1759	. . .	42
5. F. W. de Marshall	. . . .	56
6. Salem, 1766	. . . . . .	61
7. Friedberg, 1772	. . . . .	69
8. Friedland, 1780	. . . . .	73
9. Hope, 1780	. . . . . .	77
10. Revolutionary War	. . . .	80
11. Half a Century, 1803	. . . .	96
12. Salem Female Academy, 1804	. .	113
13. Indian Mission, 1801	. . . .	132
14. Negro Mission, 1822	. . . .	139
15. Home Mission, 1835	. . . .	142
16. New Congregations, 1830	. . .	149
17. The older Congregations, 1806—1856	. .	154

CONTENTS.

PAGE

18. LIST OF MINISTERS AND OTHER BRETHREN IN THE SERVICE OF THE PROVINCE IN GENERAL, AND OF THE SALEM CONGREGATION IN PARTICULAR 165
19. MINISTERS OF THE COUNTRY CONGREGATIONS . 169
20. THE BRETHREN'S UNITY 172

APPENDIX.

1. FIRST SETTLERS 179
2. CHURCHES AND PUBLIC BUILDINGS . . . 191
3. HOUSES BUILT IN SALEM 196
4. ADDITIONS AND NOTES 200

THE MORAVIANS IN NORTH CAROLINA.

I.

NORTH CAROLINA IN 1752.

IN 1749 the British Parliament passed an act by which the Unitas Fratrum, or Unity of the Brethren, was acknowledged as a Protestant Episcopal Church. By this act the free exercise of all their rights as a *church* was secured to the Moravian Brethren throughout Great Britain and all her colonies, a privilege which they did not then fully enjoy in any other European kingdom, and which is still denied to the church in certain other countries, even to the present day.

During the protracted deliberations of the Parliament, which lasted from February 20th to

June 6th, and by means of many public documents collected in a folio volume as *Acta Unitatis Fratrum in Anglia*, the attention of members of the Parliament, and other men of high standing, was repeatedly drawn to the Moravians, both as a church organization and as a social body. The testimony which Thomas Penn, proprietor of Pennsylvania, had given them in 1747, when the first act of Parliament was granted in their behalf, was abundantly confirmed, that they had conducted themselves as a sober, quiet, and religious people, and had made many improvements in their settlements which eventually would prove beneficial to the whole colony of Pennsylvania. Hence it seemed desirable to induce them to make settlements in other countries also, and invitations and offers of various kinds soon came in greater numbers than could be complied with, for want of means and men. Some of these, referring to Nova Scotia and Maryland, were not entertained at all. Another one of the Duke of Argyle, who wished a settlement of the Brethren in Scotland, led to no results; another of Lord O'Neil led, in 1764, to the settlement of Gracehill, in Ireland. But, for the present, the most acceptable offer seemed that of Lord Granville, President of the Privy Council, who was the owner of a very large tract of land in North Carolina, of which he offered Count Zinzendorf 100,000 acres on very reasonable terms.

At a conference of the Brethren, held in Lindsay-house, London, November 29th, 1751, it was resolved to accept this offer. The leading idea of Count Zinzendorf was the following: He desired that his Brethren might not only have an opportunity to be of spiritual benefit to such persons as in process of time might settle in their neighborhood, as well as to gain access to various tribes of Indians, such as the Cherokees, the Catawbas, the Creeks, and the Chickasaws, but his main object was to acquire the possession of a larger tract of land where the Moravians might live undisturbed, having the liberty of excluding all strangers from their settlements. For this purpose it was resolved not to make the good quality of the land the principal object, nor to buy detached parcels of the best land, but rather to select an undivided tract of about

100,000 acres. In the centre of this territory of the Brethren a town was to be laid out, containing the choir-houses for single brethren, single sisters, and widows, the educational institutions, and mercantile establishments. In this central place were also to be located a preparatory school for ministers and missionaries, and the directing boards for the outward and spiritual affairs of the Brethren in this their own and independent country. Besides this one town, the rest of the territory was to be parcelled out to farmers belonging to the Brethren's Church. According to an old plan in our possession, the little capital of this new Moravian country was to be built in a circular form, the eight-cornered church to form the centre, to be surrounded, in a large circle, by six choir-houses, an apothecary-shop, and a Moravian inn (*Gemein Logis*), between which buildings were to radiate eight streets, each with twenty town-lots, to be interspersed with gardens and rows of shade-trees in double circles.

This was the plan made in London by Count Zinzendorf and other Brethren, to whom North Carolina was *terra incognita*—an utterly unknown country. In order to select a tract suitable for the intended settlement, Brother Spangenberg, who was well acquainted with American affairs, was sent in 1752 to reconnoitre the country and act according to his own judgment. But before we accompany him on this journey, we will add a few words concerning

THE POLITICAL AND SOCIAL CONDITION OF NORTH CAROLINA IN 1752.

North Carolina may justly be called the *Old North State*, containing within its borders the spot on which the first Anglo-Saxon ever landed; for in July, 1584, two ships fitted out by Sir Walter Raleigh, and commanded by Philip Amidas and Arthur Barlow, dropped their anchors on the sandy beach of Roanoke Island (now Currituck County, North Carolina), and the land was formally taken possession of in the name of "Elizabeth of England, as rightful queen and princess of the same." It was called *Virginia*, in honor of the virgin queen. The first settlement on Roanoke Island, attempted in 1585, was soon after abandoned, and no permanent settlement established there until 1658.

Before this occurred, however, various parts of the present State of North Carolina had been explored by the settlers of Virginia, and here and there might be found, in the midst of friendly Indians, small clearings of the white man, who had fled the religious persecution of his native country or the tyranny of a colonial governor.

In 1663, King Charles II. granted, by a patent of March 24th, a part of Virginia, viz., "all the country between the Atlantic and Pacific Oceans, between 31 and 36 parallels of latitude," in his honor to be called *Carolina*, to eight noblemen. These eight proprietors were—

Edward, Earl of Clarendon;
George, Duke of Albemarle;
William, Earl of Craven;
John, Lord Berkeley;
Anthony, Lord Ashley;
Sir George Carteret;
Sir John Colleton;
Sir William Berkeley.

These proprietors for a long time appointed the governors, by whom the colonies were sometimes well, sometimes ill managed, but still continued to increase in numbers and to expand in cultivated lands. By the influence of Lord Granville, son of Sir George Carteret, who died in 1696, the General Assembly passed a law in 1704, by which the Church of England was acknowledged as the established church of the colony, and received privileges which were denied to all dissenters. This intolerant law produced frequent tumults among the people. In the beginning of the next century a new element was introduced into the colony by the arrival and settlement of a considerable number of Germans and Swiss. Of the 30,000 Germans who had left their own country to seek their fortunes in the Far West, about 18,000 eventually settled in North Carolina. About the same time, Christopher, Baron de Graffenreid, received a grant of 10,000 acres of land on the Neuse and Cape Fear Rivers, and settled there a body of 1,500 Swiss emigrants, by whom the town of New Berne was founded. The seat of government was at that time in Edenton, called so in 1720 in honor of Governor Eden.

In 1725 the boundary-line was run between North Carolina and Virginia, and in 1738 the southern borders were more clearly defined, the people of South Carolina having already in 1719 revolted from the feudal sway of the lord proprietors, and expelled their governor. Westward the extent of this colony was as yet quite undefined.

Both on account of the rebellion of the South Carolinians, and also on account of the comparatively small revenues to be derived from these transatlantic estates, the lord proprietors accepted the proposals of the home government, and in 1729 surrendered their claims to the crown, receiving in return the sum of 2,500 pounds sterling each. Only John, Lord Carteret, Baron of Harnes, afterwards Earl of Granville, concluded to retain his eighth part, which was laid off for him in 1743, adjoining Virginia. It is rather doubtful whether Lord Granville ever fully understood the extent of his American possessions, which were bounded on the north by the Virginia line, on the east by the Atlantic, on the south by a line in latitude 35° 34'' from the Atlantic to the Pacific Ocean, and on the west by the Pacific.

The number of inhabitants of North Carolina in 1729 scarcely amounted to 10,000, mostly scattered along the coast, in the three counties of Albemarle, Bath, and Clarendon.

The immense territory of Lord Granville was for the most part an uninhabited and utterly unknown wilderness. In 1746 Granville County was formed, and Anson County in 1749, which two counties contained the greater part of Lord Granville's vast possessions. In 1753 Rowan County was formed from parts of Anson County, and comprehended most of the western part of the present States of North Carolina and Tennessee, covering the valley of the Yadkin, and extending to or even beyond the Mississippi.

II.

WACHOVIA.

Bishop Spangenberg having accepted the appointment of selecting in the trackless wilds of western Carolina a tract of land of sufficient extent for the purposes intended, left Bethlehem, in Pennsylvania, on the 25th of August, 1752. He was accompanied by the brethren, Henry Antes, Timothy Horsefield, Joseph Miller, Herman Loesch, and John Merk, all on horseback. In Edenton, where they arrived September 10th, they were joined by Mr. Churton, the surveyor-general and agent of Lord Granville. They directed their course to the Catawba River, which they reached by the end of October, after great hardships. They had suffered more or less from fevers, especially Br. Horsefield, who had to be left at the last house they met, under the charge of Br. Miller. Br. Spangenberg and his three companions, the surveyor, and two hunters, were now at the end of all civilization, but, provided with bread for fourteen days, they manfully entered the forest wilderness, scarcely, however, anticipating that they would be wandering about here nearly fourteen weeks. It would be impossible to give an exact account of their wanderings in these trackless mountain regions of western Carolina. Suffice it to say that about eight weeks were spent in the wilderness, on the Catawba River, the heads of the New River, the Mulberry Fields (Vilkes), and the mountains, in fruitless attempts to make a suitable selection; for all the tracts which they surveyed proved too small for their intended purpose. Meanwhile winter had set in; their supply of provisions, though used very sparingly, was entirely consumed, and they had to rely on the exertions of the two huntsmen who had accompanied them. But even they, though well accustomed to the roving forest-life, became discouraged. Game was not as plentiful as might be expected, and the pasture for the horses became more scarce.

After three days of fasting, two deer were shot, which revived their strength and courage. Following their compass eastward, they reached the river Yadkin by the end of December, and willingly accepted the offer of some white settlers to spend a few days under their humble but hospitable roof. In their neighborhood, and by their direction, they found at last what they had been seeking for too far westward in vain—a larger tract of rolling woodland, well watered, and apparently well adapted for their plans.

December 27th, 1752, at the southwest corner of the Wachovia tract, the surveyors commenced, and continued to January 13th, 1753. The tract, surveyed in fourteen parcels, contained 78,037 acres. Br. Spangenberg and his companions having returned to Pennsylvania, Mr. Churton subsequently surveyed five other parcels, amounting with the other to 98,985 acres. The whole tract was called *Wachovia*, or Wachau—the *Aue* (meadow-land) along the *Wach* (the principal creek) bearing some resemblance, on account of its watercourses and meadow-lands, to a valley in Austria of the same name, which formerly was in possession of the Zinzendorf family.

On August 7th, 1753, John, Earl of Granville, the proprietor, conveyed, according to the desire of Zinzendorf, by nineteen deeds, the title of this tract, lying in the forks of Gargalee or Muddy Creek, Rowan County, to *James Hutton*, of London, secretary of the *Unitas Fratrum*, or United Brethren.

By dividing and subdividing the large county of Rowan, this tract has been successively in Rowan, 1770 in Surry, 1789 in Stokes, and since 1848 in Forsythe County.

The purchase of Wachovia coinciding in time with the great financial embarrassments of the Brethren in England, precluded the possibility of their paying the purchase-money. In order to obviate this difficulty, and because the American Brethren were yet too poor to take the responsibility upon themselves alone, it was resolved to form a *land company*, with the view of opening subscriptions among the members and friends of the Brethren, in order to obtain funds for the payment of the land, the discharge of the annual quitrent, the expenses of the first settlement, the transportation of colonists from Pennsylvania and Europe, &c. The subscribers were to be reimbursed for their advances by receiving tracts of land in Wachovia, containing each 2,000 acres, provided they further bound themselves to contribute, *pro rata*, to the wants of the colony for five years from the time of its establishment. It was expected that the enhanced price of the land would eventually repay the outlays.

On December 18th, 1753, Br. Spangenberg and Cornelius van Laer in Holland were appointed directors of this company.

Subscribers were obtained, though not as many as had been anticipated, and the purchase was effected. The centre of the tract was reserved for the Moravian settlements, and the whole plan gradually carried out in its main features, as will be shown in the sequel. For this purpose, F. W. de Marshall came to reside in North Carolina in 1768, as attorney of J. Hutton.

In 1779, *Fred. Will. de Marshall*, the administrator of the estates of the Unity in Wachovia, became the legal proprietor of all the lands of the Brethren in North Carolina, James Hutton having by deed conveyed Wachovia to Marshall. This transfer occurred during the revolutionary war, and fears being entertained that by the confiscation act of North Carolina (1777) the legal title might be invalidated, Hutton being an alien, the General Assembly of North Carolina in 1782 revested in F. W. Marshall, his heirs and assigns forever, the Wachovia tract and all other lands in North Carolina which had been acquired by the Brethren.

After the death of F. W. Marshall, in 1802, the following Brethren held the office of administrator of the Unity Estates in Wachovia:—

Christian Lewis Benzien, 1802—1811;

Lewis D. de Schweinitz, 1812—1821;

Theodore Schultz, 1821—1844;

Charles F. Kluge, 1844—1853.

His successor, Emile A. de Schweinitz, is the present administrator.

III.

FIRST SETTLEMENT AT BETHABARA.—1753.

THE necessary preparations for forming a settlement in the distant forest wilds of the South having been completed, a company of twelve single Brethren set out from Bethlehem, Pa., October 8th, 1753.[1]

---

[1] Zuvor wurden sie durch Pr. Petrus (P. Böhler) der Gemeine segnend empfohlen, und ihnen dabei zugerufen:—

"Willst du kleine Kreuzes Caravane
  Wirklich schon von hinnen zieh'n,
Nach dem dir bestimmten richt'gen Plane,
  In den Nord von Caroline?
Willst du dorten auch das Land erfreuen,
Seel' und Glieder williglich herleihen,

Among these we mention especially—

Bernhard Adam Grube, who was the first minister of the infant settlement. He had received ordination in Germany in 1740, had been actively and variously employed in Pennsylvania, and, after his return from Carolina, served there again as minister of different congregations till 1792. He died in 1808, at the advanced age of ninety-two years and nine months. As late as 1806, he expressed, in a letter to the father of the writer, the great interest which he took in the affairs of the Wachovia settlements. On his ninetieth birthday he ventured to walk from Bethlehem to Nazareth, a distance of ten miles, and a few days after returned on foot.

Jacob Lösch, the great-grandfather of the Lash family of Forsythe County, born in the State of

> Ihm zu bauen eine Stadt,
> Nach dem Grundriss, den er hat?
> Nun so benadige dich der Vater" u. s. w.

Nach dem Kelch der Danksagung wurde ihnen der Kuss des Friedens ertheilt, dass sie fühlen konnten: "Die Herzen der Gemeine sind wahrhaftig mit ihnen."

New York, where his father had arrived in 1710, was intrusted with the management and superintendence of the colony in its temporal affairs. He returned to Pennsylvania in 1769, and died in 1782.

Hans Martin Kalberlahn, a Norwegian by birth, arrived in Bethlehem in September, having lived for several years in Herrnhaag, and cheerfully accepted the appointment of surgeon and medical adviser to the first settlers. He died in 1759.

The other nine Brethren were farmers and mechanics, mostly immigrants from Europe.

They were accompanied by the Brethren Nathaniel Seidel and Joseph Haberland, from Bethlehem, and Gottlob Königsdörfer, who was on a visit in Pennsylvania from the European congregations.

Their route led through the western part of Virginia. In a wagon with six horses they carried with them various articles needed on a long journey over roads seldom travelled. To provide food for their horses, some of their number would go to the different farms, sometimes ten miles off their road, and help to thresh the oats, besides paying its full value. Not unfrequently they had to unload, and carry a portion of the load over the mountains. Sometimes the night set in before this task was accomplished, and thus the company became separated, some passing the night in the wagon, others sleeping under their tent. They generally prepared their frugal morning meal at three o'clock, and started by the dawn of day, after their regular morning prayer. Travelling by Winchester and Augusta Court-House,[1] Va., a small town of twenty houses in the mountains, after crossing the Blue Ridge at Evan's Gap, and passing the Upper Sauratown, they arrived on the 13th of November on the northern line of North Carolina. On Saturday, the 17*th of November*, at three o'clock P. M., they reached the spot where stands to this day the town of *Bethabara*, now commonly called *Old Town;* thankful to the Lord for his gracious help and protection vouchsafed unto them during

[1] Now Staunton.

their long and toilsome journey of nearly six weeks.

Here they found shelter in a small cabin, built and previously inhabited by a German of the name of Hans Wagner, but then unoccupied. Though this cabin was very small, scarcely affording room for all to sleep in (Br. Königsdörfer, in his hammock, being suspended over the heads of the others), still, they were thankful for even this scanty shelter, and resolved to remain here for the present. The daily word of the church, appointed for the day, seemed very appropriate: I know where thou dwellest, Rev. ii. 13, even in a desert place. To which was added the admonition, Be ye of one mind. In the evening, when keeping their first love-feast,[1] they were forcibly reminded that it was a wilderness

---

[1] Br. G. Königsdörfer opened the evening meeting with the following verse:—

"Wir halten Ankunftsliebesmahl
   Im Carolin'schen Lande,
  Mit einer led'gen Brüderzahl,
   Die Er zum Pilgerstande

(*ein wüster Ort*), for they heard the wolves howling round about their cabin.

The next day, being Sunday, was a real day of rest to the weary pilgrims; but on the following day they cheerfully went to work, some sharpening their axes and preparing their hoes, others beginning to construct a bakeoven, one exploring the country to find a mill where they might buy some corn, &c., whilst the three clerical Brethren (N. Seidel, Königsdörfer, and Grube) were busy in the house, preparing a kind of garret with rough boards, where they could store their goods.

Perceiving that the country was very thinly inhabited, and that they could not rely on others for provisions for any length of time, they immediately set about clearing some land; eight acres having been selected for that purpose on the

>Gezählt hat unter Seinem Volk,
>Die alle Welt durchziehet,
>Als wie die grosse Zeugenvolk,
>Die Niemand, als Er, siehet."
>
>*Diary of Bethabara,* 1753.

19th, on the days following the clearing was effected and the ploughing done, so that on the 4th of December Br. J. Lösch was able to sow the first wheat in this hitherto uncultivated soil.

Four days after their arrival, November 21st, the Brethren celebrated the Lord's supper, on which solemn occasion the Saviour manifested his presence in their midst so graciously, that their faith and hope were greatly strengthened, notwithstanding the prospect of many trials and difficulties awaiting them in the prosecution of their labors. Difficulties of various kinds were not wanting. The Brethren N. Seidel, Königsdörfer, Haberland, and Lisher having left them for Pennsylvania, December 19th, the remaining eleven Brethren made preparations for the coming winter. One was despatched to bring salt from Virginia, a distance of forty miles; another went to the Dan River to buy oxen for winter use; while several took a two days' journey to the Yadkin, to buy flour and corn. They occasionally supplied themselves with game, such as the deer and wild turkey, and not unfrequently the present of a bear was received from a neighbor. Beaver, though scarce, were sometimes trapped, and wolves and panthers were often heard close by at night. On January 1st, 1754, their little cabin caught fire, which was providentially discovered, and extinguished before much damage was done. A week later, one of their number was nearly killed by a falling limb whilst felling a tree. .The greatest difficulty, however, was the want of house-room in their small cabin, which scarcely sufficed them, and proved quite too small when travellers wished to stay over night; those who were invalids being attracted by the medical and surgical skill of Br. Kalberlahn, which was soon in great demand in the whole neighborhood, even to a distance of sixty miles. Money being scarce in the country, the Moravian doctor was paid in provisions of various kinds, or live stock, which materially assisted them in their general housekeeping. Their tailor, Br. Peterson, was also soon brought into requisition by the wants of the scattered settlers, who hitherto, if not destitute of clothing, were still in considerable straits, as their original stock was nearly exhausted, and the use of the needle and the loom not yet introduced among them. One day, for instance, a young man by the name of John Williams, living seven miles distant, brought several deerskins, instead of linsey woollen, for his needful nether-garments. In order to be able to afford their visitors better accommodations, a second cabin was erected, with a shed of split rails and posts to serve as general sleeping apartments. The garden was laid out and fenced in, and roads cut through the woods. Thus passed the first winter of the Moravians in North Carolina.

In April, 1754, quite unexpectedly, in company with John Lisher (who returned from Pennsylvania), Br. *John Jacob Fries* arrived, being successor of Br. Grube, who was recalled to the North. Br. Fries, who was born in Denmark, where, previous to his emigration, he had officiated as an assistant minister, and was known as an accomplished scholar, especially in the Hebrew language, was nevertheless a very humble servant of the Lord, ready to do the meanest service for his Brethren, and peculiarly adapted for such a station in the wilderness. He often

FIRST SETTLEMENT AT BETHABARA—1753.

referred to that time which he spent in this patriarchal housekeeping, amidst many toils and great privations, as the happiest period of his life. Utterly averse to all formality, he preferred to be a free servant of the Lord, instead of accepting any permanent appointment. He assisted in preaching and teaching whenever and wherever he thought he could be most useful, even unto his eightieth year. He died in 1798. (One day a stranger arrived, embraced the Brethren most affectionately, and said that he also was a Brother and a servant of the Lord, Charles Wesley by name. Br. Fries had his doubts about the truth of this story, and, after listening for a while to his religious professions, advised him in future rather to make horses and cows the subject of his conversation, which would suit him better, and do less harm to others.) He had scarcely gone, when a friend of the Brethren, from the Yadkin, came to inquire how this pretender had been received by them; confirming what Br. Fries had suspected, that he loved whisky more than his Saviour.

In September, Bishop P. Böhler arrived, accompanied by Br. Höger. During his stay, the name of *Bethabara* (house of passage, John i. 28, 2 Sam. xix. 19) was given to the new settlement; still keeping in view, at a future day, the founding of a more central settlement, although it was resolved, for the present, to continue their present improvements. About this time more detailed surveys of the different parts of Wachovia were made, and on that occasion names were given to the numerous watercourses, by which some of them are still known. The Cargel Creek was called Dorothea, in honor of Countess Zinzendorf; the great Lick Fork was called Johanna, Grave Fork was called Benigna, and the whole tract in cultivation received the name of Christiansburg, as most of the settlers had come from Christiansbrun, in Pennsylvania.

Their number was increased, on October 26th, by the arrival of seven Brethren, led by Br. Christensen, who was to superintend the erection of a mill. A few days after their arrival a general muster of the militia took place. By act of Parliament, the Brethren were exempt from military duty, and their not participating caused the ill-will of their neighbors to be manifested in various ways. In order to vex the Brethren, the piece of meadow-land, just sown with grass, was selected and used for military exercises, which compelled the Brethren to repeat their work upon the land, and even to procure new seed from Pennsylvania. Some of the horses became frightened, and were not recovered until a week after. The Brethren meanwhile continued their daily labor, and found opportunities to sell different articles, and thus to create a market for themselves.

The necessity of erecting a suitable building having become more urgent by the arrival of these seven Brethren from Pennsylvania, on the 26th of November, 1754, the corner-stone of the first house erected by them in North Carolina was laid with due solemnity, thus providing for a habitation where these Brethren, all being unmarried, might live together in Christian fellowship. On the 11th of March this building (a log house) was dedicated, during a visit of Bishop David Nitschman and Christ. Thomas Benzien, and soon after the Brethren moved into it.

It appearing desirable, according to the then existing customary division of the country, to have the district of Wachovia formed into a separate parish (for a separate county the number of inhabitants was too small), Br. Christ. Thomas Benzien, secretary of the Wachovia Land Company, went to New Berne and obtained an act of Assembly, by which this district was declared a separate parish, by the name of Dobbs Parish, which name was retained until the year 1776.

In the course of this year (1755) the number of inhabitants was increased by the arrival of twenty-three single Brethren and seven married couples, among whom was *Chr. Heinr. Rauch*, the first missionary among the Indians, as their spiritual guide. In the mean time the building of a grist-mill had been commenced, as well as a dwelling and meeting-house, the corner-stone of which was laid on October 25th.

Both buildings were finished in the course of 1756, the former proving of great advantage, not only to the inhabitants of the place, but to the whole neighborhood, both then, and subsequently in times of scarcity. The seven married couples moved into the new building in February, and here, on May 11th, the first child was born in Bethabara, and in holy baptism received the name of Anna Johanna Krause. In August, Bishop M. Hehl paid a visit, and introduced Br. *Christian Seidel* as German minister of Bethabara, while Br. *Gottlob Hofman* had the especial charge of the single Brethren, in Br. Fries's place, who had returned to Pennsylvania. Br. C. H. Rauch being appointed missionary for Jamaica, Br. and Sr. *David Bishop* assisted in the special care of souls among the married people.

The number of colonists was further increased by new arrivals from Pennsylvania, amounting at the close of 1756 to sixty-five persons (eighteen married people, forty-four single Brethren, one boy, and two infants).

Thus, the first difficulties of a new settlement in the forest having been overcome, more prosperous times could reasonably be expected.

IV.

INDIAN WAR.—BETHANIA.
1759.

The favorable prospects of the colony were for several years disturbed by the breaking out of the Indian war generally called the Old French War. This commenced in the northern colonies in 1755, and also affected the Brethren, ten Brethren and Sisters being murdered on the Mahony, November 24th, 1755. Gradually it spread more to the south. In 1756 it was found expedient to fortify the new settlement by surrounding it with palisades, whence it was commonly called the Dutch Fort. The mill was also fortified in a similar manner. These fortifications, rude and imperfect as they no doubt were, soon became very important for the whole neighborhood. Many fugitives, even from distant parts of Virginia, there found a place of refuge and a temporary home, and at the same time an opportunity to hear the word of eternal life. Some of these afterwards entered into a more close connection with the Brethren. As yet there was no real danger. Occasional detached companies of Cherokee warriors, as also several bodies of Creek and Catawba Indians, passed through the settlement, or encamped near the mill. Receiving plenty to eat, they behaved very well, and gave no cause for complaint. Sometimes they were accompanied by British officers, who paid for them. At other times, coming alone, with a passport of the English government, they were freely received and hospitably entertained (the government of North Carolina afterwards remunerating the Moravians). In consequence, Bethabara became a noted place among the Indians, as the "Dutch Fort, where there are good people and much bread." Br. Ettwein, who had come from Bethlehem on a visit in 1758, took an especial interest in them, and asked a company of sixty warriors whether they would like it if some of our young people should come to their country to learn their language; to which they replied that they would be proud of it, it would be a very good thing. In 1757 and 1758 more than five hundred Indians passed through the settlement at various times.

With Br. Ettwein, Br. *Jacob Rogers* arrived in Bethabara in July, 1758, having been appointed the first English minister of Dobbs Parish. He was a deacon of the Episcopal Church, had come to this country in 1752, and served as Moravian minister in Philadelphia and New York, and in Wachovia till 1762, when he returned to England.

In consequence of the war, a famine prevailed in parts of North Carolina and the adjacent districts of Virginia, and many people resorted to Bethabara (some even coming the distance of one hundred miles) to purchase flour. The Brethren having, with the assistance of those who had found a place of refuge with them, cleared an additional sixty acres of land, were thereby enabled to supply them at the usual price; while, at the same time, they omitted no opportunity to point out to them the necessity of providing for the wants of their souls, and seeking to obtain the bread of life. Some of these refugees, who had become concerned for the salvation of their souls under the preaching of the Gospel, applied for permission to join the church. To accommodate them, as well as others of the older settlers, who would have preferred their own housekeeping to the general family economy, the establishment of a new settlement was resolved upon. With a view to find a suitable location, Br. Spangenberg, who had arrived on an official visitation, June 3, 1759, with several others, went to the so-called "Walnut Bottom," about three miles northwest of Bethabara, and there, on the 12th of June, selected the spot on which the settlement was to be formed. Thirty town-lots and two tracts of bottom-land were at once surveyed and marked off by Br. Reuter, as well as a number of acres of upland for gardens and orchards, and about two thousand acres set apart for the use of this congregation, to which the name of *Bethania* was given.

It was resolved that eight married couples of the Bethabara congregation should form the nucleus of this new settlement, and should be supported for a year, until their houses could be built and some land brought into cultivation. The names of these first settlers, who built the lower part of the village, were—

>Gottfried Grabs, John Beroth,
>Balthasar Hege, Adam Kramer,
>Charles Opiz, Michael Ranke,
>Christopher Schmidt, Henry Bieffel.

They began felling trees on July 10th, on the 15th the lots were distributed by lot, and on the 18th Br. Grabs with his wife occupied the first cabin erected there; the daily word on that day being, I will fear no evil, for thou art with me, Ps. xxiii., which proved a word of much comfort to them amidst the horrors of a cruel war, and the consequent necessity of being on the alert both day and night.

Besides these Brethren, eight neighbors were allowed for the present to occupy a number of lots in the upper part of the new settlement. These were—

>Martin Houser, and his two married sons,
>George and Michael Houser;

Henry Spoenhauer;
John Strup;
Philip Shaus;
Frederick Shore, a widower, and his son,
Henry Shore.

In 1760, Br. D. Bishop moved to Bethania, to keep the daily meetings.

About the time when the new settlement was commenced, and all was bustle and activity in the Black Walnut Bottom, an alarming sickness broke out in Bethabara, which proved fatal in many cases. In quick succession were called to their eternal home, Sr. Mary Rogers, wife of the English minister; Sr. Maria C. Seidel, and her husband, Christ. Gottfried Seidel, the German minister, only forty-one years old; Hans Martin Kalberlahn, the doctor; and five other single Brethren and one married Sister—mostly after a sickness of only three or four days. Fourteen more were very ill, expecting their departure also, and twenty had a less serious attack of the same fever. There were but nineteen who entirely escaped this epidemic. As their physician had been one of the first who departed, Br.

Spangenberg became not only the spiritual, but also the medical adviser of his Brethren.

In Br. Seidel's stead, *John Ettwein*, who had returned to Pennsylvania, was recalled to Wachovia. Accompanied by his wife, they accomplished the long and tedious journey on horseback. During the trip, Br. Ettwein suffered much from a severe attack of fever. For the space of nine days he was daily compelled to lie upon the ground five or six hours, losing all consciousness from the severity of the fever. Sr. Spangenberg was also sick for several months, which obliged her husband to remain longer than he had intended. This was very fortunate, as he proved the very man to advise and direct his Brethren in the real difficulties and dangers of the Indian war, which recommenced in October, 1759.

The Cherokees and Creeks having declared war against all the white people, and murdered seven persons near Fort Loudon, the North Carolina militia was ordered to assemble in Salisbury, in November, 1759. The Brethren being exempt from military service, remained on their land, and Br. Lösch received a commission as captain of the "Dutch Fort" and governor of the watches in Bethabara and Bethania. Almost daily, either Br. Spangenberg or Br. Ettwein, accompanied by some Brethren, went to Bethania, one going and remaining there, the others returning. "On one occasion," Br. Ettwein relates (probably in March, 1760), "when early in the morning the tracks of Indians had been observed, the accompanying Brethren were rather fearful, because we generally rode quite slowly, and were talking among themselves how they might make Spangenberg ride faster. When they came to the dense woods, where the most danger was to be apprehended, Spangenberg said: 'You don't know how to ride; let me lead.'" Saying which, he set off at full speed, never stopping till they came to Bethania. There Spangenberg remained, whilst he returned to Bethabara, but was treated with less ceremony. "'It is not yet safe,' my companions said; 'we must ride as fast as we can; Spangenberg has also done so;' and thus we were racing day after day." It was subsequently proved that this precaution, as well as the orders of Br. Spangenberg to have the church-bell rung every morning at dawn of day, was not needless. Often in the morning the traces of Indians were found quite near the houses, and it was afterwards ascertained, through some who had been prisoners among the Indians, that one hundred and fifty of their warriors had encamped for nearly six weeks about six miles from Bethania, whilst a smaller camp was only three miles distant. Several times they were on the point of attacking the Fort of the Dutch, but when they came near they heard the big bell, a sign that they had been discovered. Their design of taking prisoners between the old and new town had also been unsuccessful; "for," as they expressed it, "the Dutchers had big, fat horses, and rode like the devil." Thus, under the kind providence of God, no assault was made upon either of the two settlements; but still a strict watch was kept by day and night, the new burying-ground, which was cleared in December, 1757 (being situated on the top of a very high hill), proving a very convenient place for this purpose.[1]

[1] Hence called the *Gutberg*.
The following hymn was composed by Br. Ettwein for the watchman, March 27, 1760:—

"Die Loosung hiess: 'Sie hielten Wacht
Um's Hause Gott's auch in der Nacht.'
Da fall'n mir die Liturgi ein
Die Brüder, die bestellet sein
Zu wachen um uns in Bethabara
Und auch die draussen in Bethania.

"Ich wünsche Jedem, der da wach't
Um die Gemein', bei Tag und Nacht,
Ein klares Aug', ein leises Ohr,
Ein muthiges Herz, wenn was kommt vor,
Und dass eines der starken Engelein
Mag immer mit ihm auf dem Posten sein.

"So wird, wenn auch des Satans Heer
Der Wilden zehnmal stärker wär',
Und Satan käme selber mit
Zu attaquiren unsere Hütt',
Doch unser Häuflein in der Ruh' nicht stören,
Dieweilen wir in Jesu Reich gehören.

During this time, a man wounded by the Indians arrived in Bethabara, with two arrows still in his body. He had started out, accompanied by two others, to obtain provisions from some of the neighbors, but suddenly they found themselves surrounded by Indians, who, after discharging their guns without effect, attacked them with bows and arrows. His two companions were killed upon the spot; he himself, however, escaped, and, though thus wounded, reached and forded the Yadkin River, but, meeting Indians on the opposite side, recrossed the stream, and, after losing his way and wandering about twenty-four hours in the woods, he arrived at the Dutch Fort, where Br. Lash extracted the arrows, one of which had nearly pierced him through.

A Baptist preacher, John Thomas, was killed near Abbot's Creek by the Indians. In a short

> "Wenn Gott nur immer mit uns ist,
> So kann uns keines Feindes List,
> Noch Zorn und Macht hier etwas thun,
> Wir können sanft und selig ruh'n;
> Denn seine starken Helden halten Wacht
> Und unsere Brüder geben treulich acht."

space of time no less than fifteen persons were murdered in the neighborhood.

A fall of snow in March caused the enemy finally to retire, whereby quiet was restored, so that the blessed season for commemorating the Saviour's sufferings, death, and resurrection proved a time of rich spiritual enjoyment. On Easter-Sunday a company of Orange County riflemen, sixty persons, arrived, and requested Br. Spangenberg, as the German preaching was just closed, to preach again for them, in the English language, with which request he cheerfully complied, selecting Acts ii. 36 for his text. The whole company, having laid down their arms before the house, listened with awe and attention to the fatherly admonition of the venerable Bishop, whose words seemed to make a deep impression on many.

On April 27th, Br. Spangenberg finished his labors in Wachovia, and returned again to Pennsylvania. He left for Europe in 1762, where he served the Brethren's Unity as an active and influential member of the Unity's Elders' Conference, nearly thirty years. He died in Berthelsdorf, in Saxony, September 18th, 1792, at the advanced age of eighty-eight years.

In 1761, the war with the Indians was brought to a close. The South Carolina militia having entered, near Fort Prince George, the country of the Cherokees east of the mountains, burnt about eight hundred houses, and laid waste thirteen hundred acres of Indian-corn, the Indians were forced to sue for peace, while, at the same time, the transmontane Cherokees were subdued by the Virginians. The latter were assisted by North Carolina troops, and supplied with large quantities of flour from the Bethabara mill.

Peace being fully restored, in the following year (1762) a company of fifteen Brethren and Sisters arrived from Pennsylvania, by way of Wilmington, among whom were the Brethren *John Michael Graff* (died 1782 as Bishop) and *Abraham de Gammern*, both appointed to offices in this settlement. They brought with them a small organ, the first in this place, an instrument at that time little known in the colony, and also a bell for Bethania. In July, eight couples were married, among them L. G. Bachhoff, minister of

Bethania. Br. Ettwein undertook a long missionary journey as far as Charleston, preaching and holding meetings wherever opportunity offered.

At the close of the year the congregation of Bethabara numbered seventy-five, and Bethania seventy-two souls.

V.

FREDRIC WILLIAM DE MARSHALL.

In 1763, Br. Marshall was appointed Œconomius of Wachovia, *i. e.* superintendent of all the temporal and outward affairs of the Brethren in these new settlements, which office he retained until his death in 1802.

As he has certainly acted the most conspicuous part in the affairs of Wachovia, and may be called the founder of Salem, a short biographical sketch may with propriety find its place here.

His father, George Rudolph Marshall, of Herrn Grosserstaedt, was an officer in the Saxon army. Having lost his right arm in Poland, and thereby disabled for active service, he became commander of the garrison of Stolpen, and afterwards of the fortress Königstein. In the former town, Stolpen, near Dresden, Fredr. Will. de Marshall was born, February 5th, 1721. .He and his three brothers received a christian, but at the same time a very strict military education, by which he in early years was prepared for many hardships, and acquired those traits of punctuality and methodical order which were essential qualifications for his future usefulness.

His parents were desirous that he should enter the military service, or fill some office at the court of the King of Saxony. But the King of Kings had selected him for his service as a soldier of the cross, and a champion of the truth, as it is in Christ Jesus. By means of a pious tutor, named Bretschneider, he was not only led to seek the Lord, but also became acquainted with the Brethren at Herrnhut. This acquaintance was cultivated and strengthened by a visit which he made to that place whilst a student at the University of Leipzig. At the latter place he attended a meeting held by Count Zinzendorf, in which he felt the inward conviction that he would serve the Lord in the Brethren's church, for which purpose he studied the English language. At the especial invitation of Count Zinzendorf, he came to Herrnhaag in 1739, and soon after became a member of the Brethren's congregation. From this time forward he devoted all his talents to the church of his adoption, and proved himself a faithful servant of the Lord for upwards of sixty-two years.

According to his own calculation, he spent thirty-one years in the German congregations, fifteen in England, one and a half in Holland and Prussia, thirty-two and a half in North America, and fifteen months at sea.

Concerning the earlier part of his activity in Germany and England, it will suffice to say that preaching the Gospel, attending conferences and synods, and superintending the erection of large buildings (*e. g.* Lindsay-house in London), fully occupied his time, and often tasked his strength to the utmost. He took an active part in the negotiations with the British Parliament, to which reference was made at the beginning of our narrative.

In 1750 he married Hedwig Elizabeth de Schweinitz, who proved a faithful and efficient helpmate, and departed this life in 1795. His eldest daughter, Maria Theresa, married, in 1777, Hans Christian Alexander de Schweinitz, the grandfather both of the present administrator of the Unity's possessions in Pennsylvania, E. A. Früauff, and in North Carolina, E. A. de Schweinitz.

After the death of Count Zinzendorf, with whom he had been in the most intimate connection, and for years in daily intercourse, he became a member of the first Directorial Board of the Unity, and, as such, in 1761, visited Pennsylvania, to assist in dissolving the family economy existing in Bethlehem and Nazareth, and afterwards to superintend the settlement of the central town on the Wachovia tract. Being delayed by the second Indian war of 1763, he could not venture to travel south before the fall of 1764. After returning to Europe, he in 1768 removed with his family to Bethabara.

In 1775 he attended the General Synod of the church, held at Barby, in Saxony, where he was detained, on account of the revolutionary war, until 1779, when he succeeded in reaching New York, and afterwards Salem, in safety.

There he remained, active, energetic, faithful, and self-denying, in the service of his Lord and Master, to the day of his departure, which took place February 11, 1802, six days after he had finished the eighty-first year of his pilgrimage on earth.

The 14th of February—the day on which, thirty-seven years before, he had selected the site for the town of Salem—the same on which, thirty-three years before, he had reached Bethabara with his wife—was the day of his interment in the shady grove of Salem's "acre of God."

VI.

SALEM.—1766.

BR. MARSHALL had been appointed director of the secular affairs in Wachovia, and Br. Ettwein his assistant until he himself could remove to the South. It had been recommended by the General Board of the Unity that the place for the central settlement, which, by direction of the late Count Zinzendorf, previous to his departure in May, 1760, was to be called *Salem*, should be determined upon as soon as possible. Therefore, in 1765, during the temporary presence of Br. Marshall and John Frommelt, a spot was selected which seemed suitable for the intended purpose. The situation was nearly central, between the Middle Fork, or Wach, the Brushy Fork, or Lick, and the Petersbach. The daily word on that day, February 14th, was very encouraging:

Let Thine eyes be opened towards this house night and day, even toward the place of which Thou hast said, My name shall be there. 1 Kings viii. 29.

Meanwhile the number of inhabitants had been increased by new arrivals from Pennsylvania and from Europe. In 1764 two companies arrived from Pennsylvania, the first consisting of eight adult persons, the second of twelve youths, led by Br. Lawrence-Bagge, who succeeded Br. Hoffman as spiritual guide of the single Brethren. In January, 1766, the first company direct from Europe, consisting of one married couple and eight single Brethren, arrived, by way of Charleston. Four of these and four residents of Bethabara removed on the 19th of February to a log house[1] erected in the woods, for which the first

---

[1] This log house is still standing, though considerably enlarged, and used as a potter-shop.

In June, 1766, the corner-stone was laid for the first family house, which was finished in August. Br. Praezel put up his loom there, and Charles Holder commenced the saddlery business. This house is still

tree had been cut down on January 6th. On the following day, the 20th of February, Br. Reuter surveyed the ridge, and laid out the square of the future town of Salem. The names of the first settlers were—

Gotfried Praezel, from Europe.
Niels Peterson, " "
Jens Schmidt, " "
John Birkhead, " "
George Holder, from Bethabara.
Jacob Steiner, " "
Michael Ziegler, " "
Melchior Rasp, " "

Going to their solitary hut in the woods, they were so fortunate as to kill two deer, part of which Br. Peterson prepared for dinner. The first dwelling-house was finished in August.

In October and November of the same year

standing, and may easily be recognized by its dilapidated appearance.

A two-story building, commenced in the same year, and finished the next, served as a meeting-house till 1771.

two companies arrived from Pennsylvania, the first consisting of eight youths, four single Brethren, and one widower, the latter of sixteen Sisters or girls, accompanied by Br. Richard Utley, who now entered as English minister of Dobbs Parish. Previous to this arrival, Br. M. Schropp had entered upon his duties as warden, Br. A. v. Gammern having been called to his eternal home the year before.

Br. Ettwein, who had continued from time to time to visit in South Carolina, and embraced many opportunities for preaching the Gospel in the vicinity of the Congaree, Saluda, and Broad Rivers, after serving the Lord faithfully in various capacities for seven years, now returned to Pennsylvania, having been appointed a member of the General Conference at Bethlehem. At the close of the year Bethabara contained one hundred and twenty-two inhabitants, and Bethania, eighty-seven.

After the death of Br. M. Schropp, in September, 1767, the Brn. Graff, Utley, L. Bagge, and J. Loesch formed a Diaconsis Conference, and managed the secular affairs of the three settlements till Br. Marshall arrived, in 1768, accompanied by Traugott Bagge, merchant, and several other Brethren from Europe.[1]

Br. Marshall now entered permanently upon the duties of his office, and under his energetic administration of affairs the work of the new

---

[1] In 1770 four single Brethren arrived from Europe. One of these, John Klein, appointed to superintend the outward affairs of the congregation of Salem as warden, whilst on a journey to Cross Creek (now Fayetteville), was drowned in attempting to ford Little River. His body was afterwards recovered and brought to Salem. Two others, T. Nissen (afterwards minister in Friedland) and A. Brösing, experienced a remarkable preservation of their lives. Returning in a wagon from Salisbury, they found that the ferry-boat, on which they hoped to cross the river, had been taken away. The driver resolved to ford the river, though warned not to do so, as the water was very deep. They had scarcely entered, when the horses commenced swimming, and the wagon rolled over twice. The driver and three horses were drowned, but the two Brethren succeeded in gaining a footing on the top of the wagon, and remained in this perilous situation for two hours, until they were rescued by a canoe.

settlers progressed rapidly. In 1771 Br. *Paul Tiersch* arrived as the first minister of the future Salem congregation. He was soon after followed by the Brethren John Lorez and Christian Gregor, from Germany, accompanied by Br. Ettwein, from Bethlehem. These Brethren, with Br. H. C. A. de Schweinitz, from Bethlehem, had been commissioned by the General Board of the Unity to visit the congregations in North America. During this visit several important changes were made. The superintendence of the affairs of Wachovia, hitherto vested in the General Board in Bethlehem, was transferred to a separate Board of Directors constituted for this province, consisting of the Brethren Marshall, Graff, Tiersch, and Utley; and the system of common housekeeping, hitherto maintained in Bethabara, and partly in Salem, was relinquished. In 1772 a separation of the two congregations took place, the majority of the inhabitants of Bethabara removing to Salem, which now became the centre of trade and commerce in Wachovia. By these measures the original design of establishing one principal central congregation was carried out, nineteen years after the arrival of the first Brethren in Wachovia.

At the close of 1772 the congregation of Salem contained thirty-eight married Brethren and Sisters, two widows, forty-three single Brethren and youths, twenty-two single Sisters and girls, and fifteen children—one hundred and twenty persons in all.

Among the married people were the following, as first settlers in Salem:—

F. W. Marshall, director of outward affairs;
Rev. P. Tiersch, minister;
Rev. R. Utley, warden;
Dan. Schnepf;
Matthew Miksch;
George Holder;
Jacob Meyer;
Jacob Steiner;
Traugott Bagge, merchant;
John Henry Herbst;
Charles Holder;
Valentine Beck;
Philip Meyer;
Chr. Gottl. Reuter;

Jacob Bonn, physician;
J. G. Stockburger;
Gottfried Aust.

In 1773 Br. Graff moved from Bethabara to Salem. In June he had been consecrated a bishop of the Brethren's church in Bethlehem, by the Bishops M. Hehl and N. Seidel, and in October he ordained the Brethren L. G. Bachhof and J. J. Ernst deacons of the Brethren's church, the latter being appointed minister of Bethania, and the former minister of the new congregation of Friedberg.

VII.

FRIEDBERG,—1772.

In August, 1754, not quite a year after the arrival of the first Moravian settlers in Wachovia, *Adam Spach*[1] settled about three miles from the southern line of the land of the Brethren. In September (19th) he visited Bethabara for the first time, to become acquainted with his nearest German neighbors, and cut a road from his house to Bethabara. At a second visit, in December, he requested the Brethren from time to time to send one of their number to hold meetings in his house; but, for various reasons,

---

[1] *Adam Spach*, born in 1720, in Pfaffenhofen, Alsace, came in 1754 to North Carolina; died in 1801, leaving nine children. His daughter, Johanna, born in 1766, is still living at Salem.

this request could not be complied with at that time. During the first alarms of the Indian war, he and his wife were among those who took refuge in the Dutch Fort.

At his oft-repeated and urgent solicitations, Br. Bachhof visited Adam Spach on November 26th, 1758, and preached in his house, eight German families having assembled there for the purpose. The commencement was thus made, and preaching at this place continued at intervals, the number of hearers gradually increasing, and at one time considerably augmented by the arrival of some families from Pennsylvania, previously in connection with the congregations at Heidelberg and York, who now settled in this neighborhood.

A meeting-house would have been built by them at once, if they could have received any promise or assurance of receiving a stationed minister. Thus matters remained until 1766, when, in answer to their petition, they received the promise that a minister should be stationed among them, which caused them to prepare immediately for the building of a meeting-house.

During the preparations of the building, Peter Frey died, and was buried in the present Friedberg burying-ground.

The house being finished, Br. Utley consecrated the same on March 11th, 1769, and kept a love-feast for all those who desired to become members of the new congregation. On the 12th he preached publicly, and baptized two children, viz., Joseph Frey and John Walk.

They now had stated service every four weeks, and very soon fourteen married couples pledged themselves to the support of a resident minister.

Their names were—

Valentine Frey,	John Nicol. Boeckel,
Christian Frey,	Fred. Boeckel,
Peter Frey,	Jacob Graeter,
George Frey,	Martin Walk,
George Hartman,	Peter Volts,
Adam Hartman,	Adam Spach,
John Mueller,	Christian Stauber.

On February 18th, 1770, Br. L. G. Bachhof was introduced as their minister by the Brethren Graff and Utley.

In January, 1772, this society was formally

constituted a Moravian Brethren's Congregation, by the name of *Friedberg* (hill of peace), in which, besides the preaching of the Gospel and other means of grace, the sacraments were henceforth regularly administered, the first communion being held January 17th, 1772.

In 1768 (February 19th) the corner-stone was laid for a larger church, which was consecrated May 12th, 1788, and served till 1827, when the present church was finished and solemnly dedicated.

VIII.

FRIEDLAND.—1780.

In 1769, quite unexpectedly, six German families arrived from Broad Bay, in Maine. They originally belonged to a larger company of emigrants from the Palatinate and Wurtemberg, who, about the year 1738 or 39 had landed near Broad Bay and the Muscongus River, in the province of Maine. There they had settled, and founded the town of Waldoboro', so called in honor of the principal original proprietor of the soil, General Waldo. They were Protestants, either Lutherans or German Reformed, but for a long while destitute of the means of grace. Since 1762, Br. *George Soelle*, who, before he entered the church of the Brethren, had been a Lutheran pastor in Denmark, visited them from time to time. Thus they became acquainted with the Brethren, and soon began to build a meeting-house, with a view of retaining Br. Soelle there as their resident minister. But as there were legal difficulties concerning their title deeds, and they could not enjoy full religious liberty, they resolved, according to Br. Soelle's suggestion, to emigrate to North Carolina. Having been shipwrecked on the coast of Virginia, they arrived, by way of Wilmington, in November, 1769, on the Wachovia tract, poor, wayworn, and many of them in ill health.

As the Brethren had not been apprized of their intentions, no preparations had been made for them. Some found a temporary home in Bethabara, others in Salem, where some new houses were yet unoccupied. In the following year they were joined by another company of eight families, with whom Br. Soelle arrived.[1] Not wishing to remain in Salem, they resolved

---

[1] The last survivor of these first settlers, Elizabeth Hein, late Vogler, died near Friedland, April 7th, 1855, at the advanced age of eighty-five years and three months.

to commence a settlement of their own on the southeast corner of the Wachovia tract, where nine lots, of two hundred acres each, were sold to them, and thirty acres in the centre being reserved for a meeting-house and school purposes. In 1771 nine houses were finished and occupied, and the settlement received the name of *Friedland* (land of peace).

In February, 1772, the corner-stone was laid of the house destined for church and school purposes. This house was consecrated to the worship of the Lord on the 18th of February, 1775, and Br. Tycho Nissen was introduced as minister. The names of the members of this society in connection with the Brethren's church were—

John Peter and Elizabeth Kroehn,
Michael and Catharine Rominger,
Christopher Philip and Barbara Vogler,
Melchior and Jacobina Schneider,
Frederick and Salonn Kuenzel,
Michael and Elizabeth Seiz,
Jacob and Barbara Rominger,
Frederick and Anna Maria Miller,
Jacob and Margaret Hein,

Peter and Elizabeth Schnéider,
John and Catharine Lanius,
Peter and Elizabeth Fiedler,
George Frederick and Gertrude Hahn,
Jacob and Elizabeth Ried.

In September, 1780, this society, which had meanwhile increased to forty persons, received a regular constitution as a congregation in full communion with the Brethren's church.

IX.

HOPE.—1780.

As early as the year 1758, the Brethren Rogers and Ettwein had kept meetings on the southwestern borders of Wachovia, having been invited there by Christopher Elrod and John Douthit, who had enjoyed the protection and hospitality of the Brethren whilst fugitives to the "Dutch Fort" during the Indian war. They repeatedly expressed their desire of entering into a more close fellowship with the Moravian Brethren, and soon attached themselves to the congregation at Friedberg.

But as this was an entirely German congregation, they desired to have an English Brother residing in their midst. After some years, their numbers increased by the arrival of several English families from Carrol's Manor, in Maryland, where Br. Joseph Powell had preached the Gospel to them for some years. These were followed by others a year or two later, all settling in the southwest corner of the Wachovia tract, near the Muddy Creek. For the time they participated in the enjoyment of the means of grace at the neighboring congregation of Friedberg, the Brethren Utley and Soelle attending to the English part of the congregation.

In 1775 the building of a meeting-house at *Hope* was commenced, but not completed until the spring of 1780.

On the 28th of March, 1780, the house was solemnly dedicated to the worship of God, and Br. John Christian Fritz placed in charge of the little flock of Christ, which was, on the 28th of August following, fully constituted a congregation of the Brethren's church. On this day, the 28th of August, 1780, two married couples, viz., John and Mary Padgett, and Benjamin and Mary Chitty, were added to the congregation; and on the 24th of September the first children, William Pettycord and Elizabeth Ellrod, were baptized.

The holy communion was administered for the first time on October 14th, to eight communicants.

The burial-ground at Hope was laid out during the same year.

X.
REVOLUTIONARY WAR.

The Moravian Church, as a body, has always endeavored to abstain from any participation in the political movements of the different countries to which the Lord in his providence has led them. Without prescribing anything in this respect to the individual members of the church, leaving it to every one to cherish monarchical or republican sentiments, to be unbiased in his political views, the church and all its governing bodies have ever acknowledged and acted upon the plain Gospel principle of submitting themselves to every ordinance of men for the Lord's sake, 1 Peter ii. 13; and, as faithful and loyal subjects, conscientiously to obey the laws of the land in which the Lord has placed them, and to love and honor their rulers and governors.

Being conscientiously averse to bearing arms and taking oaths, they—in the earlier times of the renewed Brethren's church—would never resort to violent measures for redressing their own grievances, nor participate in any measures of this kind adopted by others.

They therefore endeavored everywhere to comply with the apostolic exhortation, that, first of all, supplications, prayers, intercessions, and giving of thanks be made for all men, for kings and for all that are in authority, that we may lead a quiet and peaceable life, in all godliness and honesty. 1 Tim. ii. 1, 2.

Moreover, in Great Britain and all the English colonies they received important privileges by the act of Parliament of 1749. It was then enacted, "That from and after the 24th day of June, 1749, every person being a member of said Protestant Episcopal Church, known by the name of *Unitas Fratrum*, or the United Brethren, and which church was formerly settled in Moravia and Bohemia, and are now in Prussia, Poland, Silesia, Lusatia, Germany, the United Provinces, and also in His Majesty's dominions, who shall be required upon any lawful occasion to take an oath in any case where by law an oath is or shall be required, shall, instead of the usual form, be permitted to make his or her solemn affirmation or declaration in these words following: 'I, A. B., do declare, in the presence of Almighty God, the witness of the truth of what I say.' Which said solemn affirmation or declaration shall be adjudged and taken, and is hereby enacted and declared to be of the same force and effect, to all intents and purposes, in all courts of justice or other places where by law an oath is or shall be required within the kingdom of Great Britain and Ireland, and also in all and every of His Majesty's colonies and dominions in America, as if such person had taken an oath in the usual form."

Furthermore it was enacted, "That every member of the said church or congregation, residing in any of His Majesty's colonies in America, who shall at any time after the said 24th day of June, 1749, be summoned to bear arms or do military service in any of His Majesty's said colonies or provinces of America, shall, on his application to the governor or commander-in-chief of the said colony or province, or to such officer or person by whom such person shall have been summoned or required to serve or be mustered, be discharged from such personal service: *Provided,* That such person, so desiring to be discharged from such personal service, contribute and pay such sum of money as shall be rated and assessed on him in lieu of such personal service, so as such sum shall be rated, assessed, and levied, and be in such proportion as is usually rated, assessed, levied, and paid by other persons residing in the same colony or province, who are by reason of age, sex, or other infirmity unable to do personal service, and who are possessed of estates of the same nature as the persons desiring such discharge."

Further it was enacted that this privilege should be extended only to those who could procure a certificate, signed by a bishop or pastor, proving their church-membership.

Now, when in 1768, by the many acts of oppression on the part of Governor Tryon, the associations of the "Regulators" were formed, the Moravians in North Carolina took no part whatever in these movements, either for or against the governor, or the Regulators. Hence they were looked upon with a suspicious eye by both parties. In 1771 civil war was fully declared. Many deserted their plantations to join the army, which was collecting near New Garden, Guilford County, to fight against the governor, and publicly declared that the Moravians, and all those who had not assisted them, should after harvest give the half of their produce to those who had done the fighting. At the same time it was insinuated to the governor that the Brethren secretly supported the Regulators.

On May 16th a battle was fought on the road leading from Hillsborough to Salisbury, five miles west of the Great Alamance River, the forces of the Regulators being about two thousand men, those of the governor eleven hundred. The action lasted about two hours, and resulted in the total defeat of the Regulators.

On his march westward, the governor reached

Bethabara on June 4th, and encamped there with his army several days. About three hundred horses enjoyed the fine crop of grass in the large fifty-acre meadow, for which, however, the Brethren were paid.

The Brethren refrained, for conscience sake, from taking any active part in the struggle for independence. But, at the same time, they were perfectly willing to bear their part of the burden imposed by the troubles of the war on the land of their adoption.

In the beginning of 1776 some from these parts joined the army collecting at Cross Creek (now Fayetteville) to oppose the Highlanders, who had come to the support of Governor Josiah Martin. During this time some wagons from the Moravian settlements were sent to Cross Creek for salt. Being seen there, the report was spread that, under the pretence of bringing salt, munitions of war had been carried up the country, and secreted in the Moravian settlements. Thereupon, after the battle of Moore's Creek, in which the Tory army was defeated, the Committee of Safety, at Salisbury, sent a commission, consisting of seven officers and sixty men, to investigate the truth of the report. February 14th and 15th the three Moravian towns were visited, and the officers had abundant opportunity of convincing themselves of the perfectly peaceful character of the inhabitants. The Brethren, on their part, gave them a written declaration that they would submit to all requirements of the existing government of the province, but should not meddle in any way with the political movements of the country. The commissioners, on their part, gave them a certificate that the rumors referred to above were ungrounded, and that no one should molest the Moravians. Soon after, Bishop Graff was cited to appear before the Committee of Safety, in Salisbury, to answer for an intercepted package from Europe; which, however, contained nothing of a political nature, but only the regular accounts of other Moravian settlements.

In 1777 the Brethren were required to take part in the military service. They objected, from conscientious motives, declaring again that they should not refuse any tax or contribution laid upon them by the existing government. This tax was a heavy burden, especially as the price of provisions was very high, corn selling at eight shillings, and salt at six pounds ten shillings per bushel.

But still more trying was the so-called "Test Act," of 1775, requiring of every one an oath of fealty to the Government of the United States, and connected with it an oath of abjuration to King George. In case of refusal, expatriation and confiscation of property was threatened.

On this account, the Brothers T. Bagge and Blum were sent in August with a petition to the State Assembly which held its sessions at Hillsborough, by which, however, only so much was obtained, that the enforcement of this act should be postponed till the following year. A Brother was sent to Bethlehem to consult with the Brethren there, who were in the same difficulties and at a loss how to act. Meanwhile many, especially the younger portion of the Moravians, voluntarily took the State oath, whilst the older and most influential members refused to do so.

Some of the neighbors, believing that the

Moravians would surely be driven from the country, began to enter different parcels of their lands, supposing that no lawful deeds were in existence; and even the town plots of Salem and Bethlehem, as also the two mills, were entered by some speculating neighbors at the rate of 50 shillings, Continental money, for 100 acres. That there was considerable danger of the Moravians losing the title of their land there is no doubt, especially as the transfer of the legal title from James Hutton, of London, to Fred. W. Marshall, a naturalized citizen of North Carolina, had taken place after the passage of the Confiscation Act of North Carolina in 1777, and the legal proprietors were, at that time, absent in Europe.

But the wisdom of this world is often confounded by the simple faith of the children of God. When the Wachovia land had been bought from Lord Granville, Count Zinzendorf, against the advice of learned men of the town, insisted on it, that the nineteen original deeds should be given to J. Hutton "in trust for the *Unitas Fratrum*," which deed of trust made it apparent now that the Confiscation Act could not well, in right and equity, be extended to the Moravian lands.

Still, it was a time of perplexity and great anxiety for those Brethren, who, in the absence of Brother Marshall, had the management of the outward affairs of the church. Meanwhile, it was a matter of great thankfulness that a petition sent to the State Assembly in Halifax, handed in by the Brethren Praezel and C. Heckewelder, in January, 1779, was favorably received, and the resolution was passed: "that if the Moravians would render the prescribed affirmation of fealty to this and the other United States of America, they should remain in the undisturbed possession of their property, also be exempt from all military service, but instead of it pay a twofold tax."

According to this decision, all the Brethren, who had not yet taken the Test Oath, by their solemn affirmation before Justice Dobson, declared their fealty to the United States, and received certificates to that effect.

To aggravate their troubles, the seasons were unpropitious, the price of provisions increased, whilst the value of the paper currency was reduced to only four pence for the dollar. Apples and peaches froze in the bud, and the wheat was greatly injured by mildew, and the corn crop in some localities totally failed. Salt was sold at eighty shillings Continental money, or forty shillings, specie, per bushel; iron at sixteen pence per pound. Besides this, the smallpox spread in Salem, brought there by a company of cavalry of the Pulaski Legion, which had remained there for several days. No less than forty persons suffered from this disease, of whom, however, only two died.

In the fall of the year, Brother Marshall arrived, having been detained in Europe by the war since 1775, and was followed in spring of 1780 by Bishop J. F. Reichel, who was sent by the General Board of the Unity on an official visitation of all the Moravian congregations in North America. By his judicious councils and fatherly admonitions, the difficulties which had arisen here, as well as in the congregations at the North from conflicting political views, were gradually overcome; and be it said, in honor of the German Brother, brought up in a monarchical country, that by his clear perception of the state of affairs, and sound judgment, he succeeded in reconciling many whose conscientious scruples had left them in much perplexity.

His labors were signally blessed by the Lord, and the harmony was restored, which is so essential to the welfare of a Christian community. During Brother Reichel's visit, the monthly conference of the ministers of the country congregations was instituted at Salem, Sept. 15th, 1780, which has been continued ever since. Friedland and Hope received their full organization as Congregations of the Brethren.

Of the incidents of the revolutionary war, the following interesting particulars have been preserved, which, in their details, prove sufficiently that our fathers conscientiously refrained from any participation whatever in it.

In June, 1780, more than a thousand Tories assembled in the neighborhood of the Moravian settlements, committing many acts of violence. To oppose them, the militia was collected everywhere, which scoured the country, taking horses, rifles, and provisions at their pleasure. The Moravian settlements were often visited. Meanwhile, 3000 Continental troops had assembled at Cross Creek, and were joined by 7000 militia, to march against the English. For their support, supplies from the newly gathered wheat were ordered, which, in Salem and neighborhood, were collected by an officer and sixty men. Wagons and horses were also taken, to convey the flour to the army. In the disastrous battle of Camden, in which General Gates was totally defeated, some of our wagons and horses were lost, of which six belonged to the Brethren of Bethania.

In August, several hundred men of the Virginia militia, as scouting parties were quartered at Bethabara. The military possession of the place lasted three weeks, causing great scarcity of provisions and suffering to the Brethren.

On Sept. 13th, Brother Fritz received at Hope a visit of sixteen horsemen, who were provided for by him.

In October, a party of 500 militia made Bethania their head-quarters. Soon after, 300 prisoners, among whom were 50 English taken near

King's Mountain, were brought and kept there nineteen days, until all provisions to be found in the place were consumed.

In 1781, the Brethren had abundant cause of appreciating the truth of the promise: He shall deliver thee in six troubles; yea in seven there shall no evil touch thee, Job v. 19. For when, in the first months of the year, the theatre of war came nearer and nearer to the Moravian settlements, still no actual hostilities occurred on the Wachovia Tract.

January 7th, 22 men, 40 horses, and 2 baggage wagons of General Greene's division were quartered in Salem, and remained there till February 4th.

January 12th, a committee of four Brethren was appointed, to care for the military affairs, by whom a barrack was erected at some distance from the town, where a military store was kept for some time. This military store, and a hospital, which had been erected in Salem, were removed on February 5th, the Friedberg and Bethania Brethren furnishing wagons. On the same day, General Pickens's corps encamped near Bethabara.

February 7th and 8th, several hundred men of Wilkes County (N. C.) and of Georgia militia passed through Salem.

On the 9th of February, the British army under Lord Cornwallis encamped in Béthania, and passed the next day through Salem and the Friedland settlement, which proved a rather expensive visit, Bethania alone losing 23 horses, 80 head of cattle, and all their poultry. Soon after the Wilkes County militia paid a second visit to Salem and Bethabara.

In November, 63 members of the Assembly, with the newly elected governor, Alexander Martin, of Guildford County, spent several weeks in Salem for the purpose of holding their session, which, however, failed for want of a quorum.

In January, 1782, this visit was repeated, and the members of the Assembly had abundant opportunity of making themselves fully acquainted with the religious and social state of the Moravian settlements.

This was important for the Brethren, and

proved of advantage in obtaining an especial Act from the Legislature of North Carolina assembled at Hillsboro', by which F. W. Marshall was duly acknowledged as the proprietor of the Wachovia Tract, and all the lands which had been acquired by the Brethren in North Carolina.

Brother Traugott Bagge was elected member of the Assembly, auditor, and justice of the peace.

In this year the faithful pastor of the Salem congregation, Brother J. M. Graff, the first bishop ever residing in any of the Southern States, departed this life.

In 1783, the solemn thanksgiving day for the restoration of peace, was celebrated on July 4th with great joy and gladness of heart, and with especial gratitude to the Lord for all his mercies and providential preservations during these trying times.

XI.

HALF A CENTURY.—1803.

EARLY in the morning of January 31st, 1781, the cry of fire disturbed the peaceful slumbers of the inhabitants of Salem. The tavern was in flames, and the inmates, Brother and Sister Meyer, with their children, and Brother Holland had barely time to escape. The kitchen building was destroyed, but the stables and other out buildings were saved. The timber and other building materials, which had been prepared for the erection, during this year, of a building for a "Single Sister's House," were now used for the re-construction of the tavern, and the erection of the sister's house deferred until the following year.

In September, 1784, Br. *John Daniel Köhler* arrived from Europe, as minister of the congregation at Salem. He was accompanied from

Litiz, Pa., by Brother *Simon Peter*, who took charge of the congregation at Friedberg.

In company with Brother Köhler from Europe were also Brother and Sister *John* and *Benigna de Watteville*, who were deputed by the General Board of the Unity to pay an official visit to all the American congregations. They sailed from the Texel (Holland), September 27th, 1783, and arrived off Sandy Hook in November, but a continuation of severe northwest storms, rendered all their attempts to land at New York fruitless, so that they finally resolved, in January following, to sail to the West Indies. On the 17th of February, 1784, they stranded on a cliff near the Island Barbuda, which they reached in boats with difficulty. The governor of the island assisted and entertained them kindly. From Barbuda they proceeded to Antigua, and thence to Philadelphia and Bethlehem, which place was reached June 2d.

After having visited all the northern congregations, *Bishop Watteville* proceeded to the south and arrived in Salem October 23d, 1785, where he remained till April 26th, 1786. During his stay, a Board of Directors for this province was recognized, and called the Provincial Elders' Conference, consisting of the Brethren Marshall, Köhler, Praezel, and Benzien. This directing Board resolved to erect at Bethlehem, a new church building, in connection with a dwelling for the minister. The site thereof having been determined upon, the corner-stone was laid on April 8th, 1785. The Lord's blessing accompanied this undertaking in such a manner, that, notwithstanding the apparent insufficiency of means, through the active Christian zeal of the people, this church-building was ready for consecration before the close of the year, its solemn dedication to the worship of the Triune God taking place November 26th, 1788. The daily word of the church: Thus saith the Lord of Hosts: My cities through prosperity shall yet be spread abroad, afforded promise of his aid and blessing in days to come. A large number from the other congregations were present on the occasion, participating in the blessing, attending the various meetings during the day. On the following Sunday, the 30th, the first public preaching was held in the new church, Brother Köhler delivering the first sermon in the German, and Brother Fritz, assistant minister in Bethabara, preaching in the English language. Many of the neighbors were present, the whole number being about 600, whose attention during service, and subsequent declarations indicated that the Spirit of God had borne testimony to the word of the cross.

The General Synod of the Brethren's Unity, held at Herrnhut, Germany, in 1789, which Br. Benzien attended as delegate of the Wachovia Conferences, resolved upon the establishment of a Moravian congregation in South Carolina. This was to be undertaken in compliance with one of the many invitations which, since the close of the war, had been extended to the Brethren to increase the sphere of their usefulness. The Hon. Henry Laurens, formerly President of Congress, and one of the commissioners for the United States at the peace of Paris, had long been well acquainted with the Brethren at Salem. Whilst visiting in Bethlehem, Pa., during the war, he held friendly intercourse with Bishop

Ettwein, and proposed to him an establishment of the Brethren in South Carolina, for which purpose he made both verbal and written promises to convey to them, by deed of gift, two thousand acres of land in the district of *Ninety-Six*.

This district embraced the northwestern part of the State of South Carolina, deriving its name from a military fort built in the Indian wars, about ninety-six miles from Orangeburg. On its site now stands Cambridge, in Abbeville District.

To comply with the direction of the General Synod, the Brethren Marshall and Benzien undertook a journey to this then wild and unsettled region in November and December, 1790. They first visited Mr. Laurens at his rice-plantation on the Cooper River, nine miles from Monk's Corner; then his partner, John Lewis Gervais, in Charleston, by whose assistance they were conveyed to the agent in Abbeville District, Major Bowie. After a difficult journey through swamps and over almost impassable roads, they reached, on December 10th, the wilds of Long

Cane Creek and Reedy Branch, where Major Bowie assisted them in selecting, from the five thousand acres belonging to Mr. Laurens, a tract of two thousand acres which seemed well adapted for a settlement, distant about twenty-five miles from the Savannah River. As the season was already far advanced, the survey could not at the time be made. They thereupon returned home, Major Bowie promising them that as soon as practicable he would have the survey completed. Before this was accomplished, however, Mr. Laurens died; and as by his last will and testament all his property was bequeathed to a grandchild, without any provision being made therein for the proposed grant and settlement, the whole plan had to be abandoned.

On May 31st, 1791, Salem was visited by the first President of the United States, *George Washington*, then on a visit to Alexander Martin, Governor of North Carolina. Gen. Washington spent a day among the Moravians, visiting the houses of the single Brethren and single Sisters, and in the evening attending service in the church. The President seemed to take an especial interest in the water-works by which the town was supplied with water.

The following address was presented to him on June 1st:—

"*To the President of the United States:*

"Happy in sharing the honor of a visit from the illustrious President of the Union to the Southern States, the Brethren of Wachovia humbly beg leave, upon this joyful occasion, to express their highest esteem, duty, and affection for the great patriot of this country.

"Deeply impressed as we are with gratitude to the great Author of our being for his unbounded mercies, we cannot but particularly acknowledge His gracious providence over the temporal and political prosperity of the country, in the peace whereof we do find peace, and wherein none can take a warmer interest than ourselves, in particular when we consider that the same Lord who preserved your precious person in so many imminent dangers has made you in a conspicuous manner an instrument in his hands to forward that happy constitution, together with those improvements whereby our United States begin to flourish, over which you preside with the applause of a thankful nation.

"Whenever, therefore, we solicit the protection of the Father of Mercies over this favored country, we cannot but fervently implore His kindness for your preservation, which is so intimately connected therewith.

"May this gracious Lord vouchsafe to prolong your valuable life as a further blessing and an ornament of the constitution, that by your worthy example the regard for religion be increased, and the improvements of civil society encouraged.

"The settlements of the United Brethren, though small, will always make it their study to contribute as much as in them lies to the peace and improvement of the United States, and all the particular parts they live in, joining their ardent prayers to the best wishes of this whole continent that your personal as well as domestic happiness may abound, and a series of successes may crown your labors for the prosperity of our times and an example to future ages, until the glorious reward of a faithful servant shall be your portion.

"Signed, in behalf of the United Brethren in Wachovia,

"FREDERICK WILLIAM MARSHALL,
"JOHN DANIEL KÖHLER,
"CHRISTIAN LEWIS BENZIEN.

"Salem, *the 1st of June,* 1791."

To which the President of the United States was pleased to return the following answer:—

"*To the United Brethren of Wachovia:*

"Gentlemen : I am greatly indebted to your respectful and affectionate expression of personal regard, and I am not less obliged by the patriotic sentiment contained in your address.

"From a society whose governing principles are industry and the love of order much may be expected towards the improvement and prosperity of the country in which their settlements are formed, and experience authorizes the belief that much will be obtained.

"Thanking you with grateful sincerity for

your prayers in my behalf, I desire to assure you of my best wishes for your social and individual happiness.

"G. WASHINGTON."

Before the close of the century, during the latter half of which the Brethren had settled in this State, the erection of a new and larger church for the increasing central congregation of Salem became necessary. The corner-stone was laid June 1st, 1798, with appropriate ceremonies. Br. Marshall superintended the erection of this building, and had the pleasure of witnessing its completion in 1800. On November 9th, 1800, it was solemnly consecrated to the worship of Almighty God; the Brethren Benzien, from Salem, and Simon Peter, of Bethania, officiating upon this occasion. Br. Köhler, who had during the space of sixteen years officiated as pastor of the Salem congregation, and since 1790 as bishop of the Brethren's church, was prevented from participating on this joyful occasion, having already set out on his journey to Europe, to attend the General Synod of the church at

Herrnhut, in Germany, in 1801. On the 13th of November, an important memorial day of the church, the holy communion was for the first time administered in the new church, the communicants of all the neighboring congregations having assembled for the purpose.

At the General Synod of 1801, Br. *C. G. Reichel*, then minister in Nazareth, Pa., and principal of the Boys' Boarding-School at Nazareth Hall, was appointed Br. Köhler's successor. He was consecrated a bishop of the Brethren's church by Bishop Ettwein, and arrived in Salem May 31st, 1802. Br. Marshall had departed this life in February of the same year. Shortly before his death he wrote a long letter to Br. Reichel, containing minute directions in reference to his journey, the provisions and other needful preparations for "camping out," &c.; an interesting document, showing that fifty years ago a journey to or from Pennsylvania was a greater undertaking than a voyage across the Atlantic in our days.

Br. Reichel entered upon his duties as pastor of the Salem congregation on June 6th, 1802, and served faithfully till April, 1811. He was at the same time president of the General Directing Board, in which were associated with him the Brethren Benzien (Br. Marshall's successor as proprietor and administrator of the Wachovia estates) and Simon Peter (minister of Bethabara).

In the year 1803, fifty years having elapsed since the arrival and settlement of the Brethren at Bethabara, in this State, the event was celebrated by a solemn jubilee, held on the 17th of November at Salem. All the members of this first congregation, with their children, were invited to repair to Salem, and the same invitation was extended to the adult members of the congregations at Bethania, Friedberg, Friedland, and Hope. Contrary to expectation, the weather on this day proved unusually pleasant for the lateness of season, so that a large number were able to attend. These met at half-past nine o'clock A. M. in the handsomely decorated church, uniting in rendering thanks and praises to that unchangeably gracious God and Saviour whose mercies had never failed throughout the half century past. Deeply bowed down before Him, who had indeed done great things for them, the voice of gladness and rejoicing broke forth, and their hearts united in covenanting anew with the Lord, and with each other, to be and to remain His faithful people. At the love-feast, held in the course of the day (of which upwards of five hundred and sixty person partook), the aged Br. John Beroth, of Bethania, one of the two survivors of the twelve Brethren who commenced Bethabara fifty years before, was present, together with his wife; Br. Grube, then eighty-eight years of age, had sent from Pennsylvania, where he then resided, a congratulatory ode composed by him for the occasion, which we insert in full:—

BR. GRUBE'S HYMN.

1. Du liebe Wachauer Gemein'!
   Ich stimm' heut' in dein Loblied ein,
   Das du zu deinem Jubelfest
   Fröhlich dem Herrn erschallen lässt,
   Für alles was Er hat an dir gethan
   Seitdem die ersten Brüder kamen an.

2. Ich war auch mit in ihrer Zahl,
   Und freu' mich noch derselb'gen Wahl,
   Da wir zwölf Brüder auf dem Land',
   Wo eine kleine Hütte stand,
   Den Einzug hielten, voller Dankbarkeit,
   Und war'n beisamm'n in Lieb' und Einigkeit.

3. Es war uns freilich alles neu,
   Und mangelte uns mancherlei;
   Wir waren aber nicht verlegen,
   Und hofften auf des Heilands Segen;
   Man hörte, denn ein Jedes war vergnügt,
   Von keinem auch die mind'ste Klage nicht.

4. Zur Arbeit musst' man sich gleich rühr'n,
   Um ein Stück Land zur Saat zu *clearn;*
   Die Kost dabei war freilich schmal,
   Allein wir hatten keine Wahl,
   Als *Hominy* war unser täglich Brodt,
   Und wir genossen's mit Dank gegen Gott.

5. Wir gingen wohl zu manchen Tagen
   Auch aus, um etwas zu erjagen;
   Allein das schlug uns immer fehl;
   Bekamen denn zum Welschkornmehl
   Doch ein'ge Kürb'se, so war's schön und gut,
   Und wir behielten immer guten Muth.

6. Denn auch an diesem wüsten Ort
   Erquickte uns des Heilands Wort;
   Wir weideten uns immer d'ran,
   Und unser blut'ger Schmerzensmann
   Erwies sich uns sehr freundlich und voll Huld,
   Und hatte mit uns Kindern viel Geduld.

7. Er selbst wusst' uns auch zu bedecken
   In mancherlei Gefahr und Schrecken.
   Bei'm Bäumefellen schien einmal
   Ein Bruder unserer kleinen Zahl
   Durch einen Ast tödtlich verletzt zu sein:
   Doch konnt' man sich bald seiner Besserung freu'n.

8. Als ich ein halbes Jahr gewest
   Bei'n Brüdern, ward ich abgelöst
   Durch unseren sel'gen Bruder Fries,
   Der sich als ein Mann Gott's bewies,
   Und sich zu allem williglich gab her,
   Und wenn's auch nur die Ruh' zu hüten wär'.

9. So wurde der Anfang gemacht.
   Man hat's damals wohl nicht gedacht
   Was unser Herr in fünfzig Jahren,
   Darunter manche schwere waren,
   Zu Seinem Lob und Preis doch hat bereit't.
   Er sei dafür gelobt in Ewigkeit!.

10. Ich wünsche nun besonders heut'
   Dass unser Heiland hätt' die Freud',
   Dass jede Seel' auf diesem Land'
   Recht innig würd' mit Ihm bekannt;
   O möchte Jedes ganz für Ihn gedeih'n!
   So wird Er sich, und wir mit Ihm uns freu'n.

11. Gott gebe dass der ganze Sinn
   Nur immer geh' auf Jesum him,
   Auf Seine Marter, Blut und Tod,
   Der uns erlöst aus aller Noth,
   Und dass die Herzen bleiben abgekehrt
   Von allem, was zur Welt, zum Fleisch gehört.

12. Mit Jésu Segen geht denn fort,
   Recht froh, ein Jed's an seinen Ort.
   Er sei Euch allen innig nah',
   Ihr mög't sein dorten oder da.
   Ja Er erhebe die durchgrab'ne Hand
   Über Euch all' auf dem Wachauer Land'!

Within fifty years there were baptized 1,357 children of the members of the six congregations, 43 adults, and about 1,300 children of friends and neighbors; 666 persons were buried at the different burial-grounds.

The whole number of church-members and children at the close of the half century presents the following

SUMMARY.

		Communicants.	Non-communicants.	Children.	Total
1.	Salem	180	27	83	290
2.	Bethabara	33	16	32	81
3	Bethania	76	95	122	293
4.	Friedberg	75	109	147	231
5.	Friedland	21	72	42	135
6.	Hope	35	66	74	175
		420	385	500	1305

XII.

SALEM FEMALE ACADEMY.
1804.

THE year 1804 was distinguished in our province by the commencement of the Salem Female Academy, which has since become well known in the Southern States of the Union, and has flourished more than fifty years. This institution, now one of the oldest in the Southern States, kept in grateful remembrance by many Christian mothers who here received their first and lasting impressions of eternal truths, and have had the satisfaction of seeing their daughters and granddaughters educated at the same place, and according to the same Christian principles. For the sake of the juvenile scholars of this institution, we have endeavored, with the kind assistance of its present principal, to collect all the dates referring to the outer history of this institution. Still more important and more instructive would be the inner history thereof, embracing the experiences made by the hundreds of little girls and young ladies who have been its inmates, and of the influence which their education in the Moravian boarding-school has had upon their after-life on earth, and upon their dying hour; but to trace their inner history would be in most cases impossible, and we, therefore, leave it to the former pupils, into whose hands this historical sketch may fall, to supply this want from their own personal recollections, feeling confident that they could do it more completely and more to their own satisfaction than we can. The following carefully collected notes, though referring only to the outer history will, we trust, not prove uninteresting.

Before the close of the last century, the wish had often been expressed by visiting friends and strangers, when seeing the educational advantages of the youth of this small Moravian town, that their children might be permitted to participate in them, and there were among the members of the Salem congregation not a few, who considered it their Christian duty to serve their friends in the Southern States, and at the same time to work in their heavenly Master's cause by raising the standard of female education.

These petitions became more urgent, and the plan received a more definite expression, after Bishop Reichel, the founder, and for seventeen years principal of Nazareth Hall,[1] had become the president of the Wachovia Provincial Conference, the directing Board of the Moravian congregations at the South. The main difficulties seemed to be the want of a suitable house for school purposes, and an adequate number of well qualified female teachers. Brother Reichel's daughter, educated in the Bethlehem Female Academy, assisted by M. S. Meinung and J. E. Praezel, who had given full satisfaction in the day-school for little girls, sufficed for the present, and among the older girls who had received private lessons from Brother C. Th. Pfohl, there also were some who could be calculated upon as suitable assist-

[1] History of Nazareth Hall, from 1755 to 1855, p. 29.

ants for the future. Taking all this into consideration, the Conference resolved, October 31st, 1802, to give to Brother *Samuel G. Kramsch*, minister of the English congregation at Hope, who, as well as his wife, had served as teachers in boarding-schools, and were well acquainted with their details, the appointment of commencing a female boarding-school at Salem.

On October 6th, 1803, the corner-stone for the building to be erected on the square between the "congregation house" and sister's house was laid with appropriate ceremonies, Bishop: Reichel conducting the religious exercises both in the meeting-hall and out-doors, in the German language.

In a copper case—inserted into the cornerstone, at the northwest corner of the building—the following inscription was deposited in the German and English languages:—

In the name of God,
the Father and the Son, and the Holy Ghost,
in the year
after the birth of our Lord and Saviour Jesus Christ
one thousand eight hundred and three,

SALEM FEMALE ACADEMY.—1804.

on the sixth day of October,
in the twenty-seventh year
of the Independence of the United States of America,
when Thomas Jefferson was President of them,
in the fiftieth year
after the settling of the first members of the Church
of the United Brethren in North Carolina and
the beginning of building Bethabara,
in the thirty-eighth year
since the beginning of building Salem,
the foundation-stone of this house
for a BOARDING SCHOOL of Girls
was laid in a solemn manner,
in the presence of the whole Congregation,
with fervent Prayer to our Lord,
that by the School, to be established in this House
His name may be glorified,
His kingdom of Grace be enlarged in this Country
and the Salvation of Souls
of those, who shall be educated therein, be promoted.

THE DAILY WORD WAS:

Believe on the Lord Jesus Christ, and thou shalt be saved, and thy house. *Acts* xvi. 31.

A dying, risen Jesus,
Seen by the eye of faith,
At once from danger frees us,
And saves the soul from death.

THE DOCTRINAL TEXT:

He had done no violence, neither was any deceit in his mouth. *Is.* liii. 9.

> May our mind and whole behaviour
> Bear resemblance to our Saviour
> And his sanctifying merit
> Hallow body, soul, and spirit.

Among some other papers preserved in the corner-stone is also a list of all the little girls belonging to the Salem congregation under 12 years of age. They were 42 in number, 23 attending school. Of these 42 girls and infants, 12 have, in the course of time, become teachers in the academy, and one of them is teaching to this day, and well remembers how she and her companions were standing by and watching father Reichel, Benzien and Kramsch, each in turn, strike three times with a mallet the stone in which the copper case was inclosed, where also her name was recorded; how Brother Reichel, standing upon the corner-stone, implored the blessing from on high upon the building undertaken in the name of the Lord for the promotion of His glory and the spiritual and eternal well-being of many immortal souls. Among the strangers attending these impressive ceremonies was a gentleman from Georgia with his little daughter, who two years after entered as the first pupil from that State.

Before the house could be finished, on May 16th, 1804, four pupils were brought from Hillsborough, and, for the present, received in some rooms of the "Congregation-house," temporarily arranged for the purpose. These were, Misses Elizabeth Strudwick, Ann and Elizabeth Kirkland, and Mary Philips. Soon after four others came, Anna and Felicia Norfleet from Halifax, Anna Steirs from Fayetteville, and Rebecca Carter from Caswell County, all from this State. To these were added Anna Pauline Shober and Mary Steiner from Salem, of which the former, Mrs. Herman, is still living here, and the latter, Mrs. Dencke, still teaches in the academy.

The first teachers, Sophia Dorothea Reichel (Mrs. Seidel), Maria Salome Meinung (Mrs. Ebbeke), and Johanna Elizab. Praezel (Mrs. Meinung), are still living, the two former in Bethlehem, Pa., and the latter in Salem.

The new house having been finished in a year and nine months, the 16th of July, 1805, was set apart as the day of its solemn consecration. The boarders, village girls, and the ministers of the different congregations having assembled at one o'clock in the prayer-hall of the congregation-house, a procession was formed by the scholars, headed by the clergy, and followed by the teachers. When leaving the house, a choir of trombones performed a solemn tune, and, entering the new house, another choir of trombones received them in a similar manner. The whole company assembled in the sleeping-hall (being the largest room in the house), in two large semicircles, the pupils all being dressed in white, and the musical choir, accompanied by a pianoforte and other instruments, sang—

> Peace be to this habitation,
>   Peace to every soul therein;
> Peace which flows from Christ's salvation,
>   Peace, the seal of cancelled sin;
> Peace that speaks its heavenly giver,
>   Peace to earthly minds unknown;
> Peace divine, that lasts forever,
>   Here erect its glorious throne.

To which all assembled there responded—

> This habitation,
>   And all who dwell therein,
> Fill with salvation;
>   O, may in each be seen
> True grace
> And lovely childlikeness.

After a fervent dedicatory prayer by Br. Reichel, a love-feast was held, according to the well-known and time-honored custom of the Brethren, in which also participated some strangers from Camden, S. C., who on that day brought their two daughters, the first pupils from South Carolina, which, next to our own State, has sent the most scholars to our academy.

The first inmates of the new house were Br. and Sr. Kramsch and their two daughters (still living), twenty boarders, and four teachers. After the usual evening meeting of the congregation, the scholars assembled once more before the house, surrounded by the whole congregation, to offer hymns of thanksgiving, praise, and prayer.

In 1806 the first printed circular was issued,

containing the "Terms and Conditions of the Boarding-School for Female Education in Salem, N. C.," from which it appears that the age of admittance was between eight and twelve years, and the age of fifteen terminated the stay of pupils at school. The yearly expenses were calculated at about $160; entrance-money, $5.

The branches taught were: Reading; grammar; writing; arithmetic; history; geography; German, if desired; plain needlework. Extra branches: Music, drawing, and ornamental needlework.

In 1806, Br. Sam. G. Kramsch was succeeded by Br. *Abraham G. Steiner*, who for ten years presided over the institution as its inspector or principal. The number of scholars increasing, a third room had to be arranged in 1807, and a fourth in 1811; when a new building was erected, as the dwelling-house for the principal and his family, and thus some room gained in the academy building. This, however, not proving sufficient, a number of boarders had to lodge in private families, which was continued for some years, until, by additions to the old building, more house-room could be gained. In 1814, seventy-four of the pupils were ill of the measles, which then was extensively prevalent in the place, in no case, however, proving fatal.

In 1816, Br. Steiner was compelled, by the failure of his health, to resign his charge, and Br. *G. Benjamin Reichel*, son of Bishop Reichel, entered as the third principal, and served the institution faithfully till his death, in December, 1833. During his term an addition was made to the academy building in 1824, containing, besides some school-rooms, a chapel, which was solemnly consecrated on September 24th, and gave rise to the so-called "chapel festival," which no doubt many scholars remember as a time of rich and lasting spiritual blessings. In 1826 the number of room companies had increased to six, representing six of the Southern States of the Union. A few years later the number had considerably decreased, partly owing to the great money pressure at the South, the erection of other boarding-schools, and the failing health of the principal.

Br. Reichel breathed his last December 20th, 1833, having been since 1816 inspector of the academy, and since 1829 also pastor of the Salem congregation.

In 1834, Br. *J. C. Jacobson*, minister at Bethania, was appointed principal of the academy, and filled the station for ten years. During his time the number of boarders again increased, and reached in 1838 one hundred and eighty, instructed by nineteen teachers. To make more house-room, a new chapel was built in 1835, and gradually one room after the other taken possession of in the old "congregation-house," until in 1841, after a new chapel for the congregation and a minister's dwelling had been built, the whole house, with its premises, was appropriated to the purposes of the school.

In 1844, Br. Jacobson accepted an appointment as principal of the Boarding-School for Boys at Nazareth Hall, Pa., and Br. *Charles A. Bleck* entered as the fifth principal.

He was succeeded, in December, 1848, by Br. *Emil A. de Schweinitz* as the sixth, and in February, 1853, by his brother, the present well-known principal, Br. *Robert de Schweinitz*. It will hardly be necessary to say anything about the present state of this institution, so extensively and so favorably known in the Southern States, and so fully patronized by the daughters and granddaughters of former pupils. But, for future reference, we will mention two dates, viz., August 9th, 1854, on which day the corner-stone of the *new academy building*[1] was laid with appropriate religious ceremonies, and March 24th, 1856, on which day the beginning was made of removing from the old to the new house. As the old building required extensive repairs, all the scholars, 216 in number, lived within the walls of the new building, besides which about 75 day scholars attended the school.

[1] For a description of the new academy building, see Appendix—Public Buildings.

The following is a list of the

RESIDENT TEACHERS OF THE SALEM FEMALE ACADEMY;

including the teachers of the village girls' school, with the time of their service. Those marked thus (†) have since departed this life. Those in Italics are still in service.

		Entered.	Left.	Remarks.
1.	Sophia Dorothea Reichel	1804	1809	Mrs. Seidel.
2.	Maria Salome Meinung	1804	1807	Mrs. Ebbeke.
3.	Johanna Elizabeth Praezel	1804	1808	Mrs. Meinung.
4.	†Joh. Sophia Shober	1805	1806	
	Re-entered	1807	1809	Mrs. Zevely.
5.	†Joh. Elizabeth Reus	1805	1816	
	Re-entered	1811	1814	
	"	1816	1820	Mrs. Ochman.
6.	†Agnes Susanna Praezel	1805	1816	Mrs. Petersen.
7.	†Mrs. M. E. Praezel, assisting in town school	1805	1813	
8.	†Barbara Leinbach	1806	1807	
9.	†Philipina Christman	1806	1820	Mrs. Summers.
10.	†Rebecca Hartman	1806	1812	
11.	Mary Walk	1806	1809	Mrs. Curtis, Norfolk.
12.	Susanna Elizabeth Peter	1807	1827	Mrs. Zevely.
13.	†Elizabeth Dans	1807	1807	Mrs. Winkler.
14.	Johanna Elizabeth Nissen	1808	1811	Mrs. Fries.
15.	Salome Fetter	1809	1814	
	Re-entered	1815	1817	
	"	1818	1819	Mrs. Friday.
16.	Maria Steiner	1811	1820	
	Re-entered	1824	1828	*Mrs. Denke.*
17.	†Henrietta Fried. Fierling	1811	1814	Mrs. Reichel.
18.	Anna Paulina Shober	1812	1817	
	Re-entered	1819	1820	Mrs. Herman.
19.	†Maria Eliz. Kummer, assisting in town school	1814	1814	
20.	†Anna Rebecca Holder	1814	1815	
	Re-entered town school	1821	1822	Mrs. Zevely.

SALEM FEMALE ACADEMY.—1804.

	Entered.	Left.
Charlotte Louisa Kramsch	1814	1831
Re-entered	1833	1837
Christina Christman, town school	1814	1820
†Elizabeth Transou	1814	1816
†Joh. Salome Christman	1816	1820
Christina Caritas Schneider	1817	1824
†Maria Theresia Shober	1817	1819
†Maria Cath. Transou	1817	1818
†Maria Fetter	1817	1818
Ruth Montgomery Rhea	1818	1820
Susanna Elizabeth Loesh	1819	1820
Henrietta Kluge	1819	1821
†Maria Belling	1820	1821
†Maria Gambold	1820	1824
†Caroline Eberhard	1820	1828
†Mary Towle	1820	1823
†Sarah Louisa Towle	1820	1825
†Wilhelmina Boehler	1820	1823
Sibylla Dull	1820	1824
†Cathar. Reich	1821	1827
Johanna Elis. Schulz, town school	1822	1824
Caroline Schulz	1822	1823
Lydia Stauber	1824	
Regina Leinbach	1824	1827
Re-entered	1829	1842
†Eliza Bagge	1824	1827
Mariam Erenstine Benade	1825	1829
†Sophia Christ. Kitschelt	1825	1827
Charlotte Friedrica Pfohl	1826	1852
Re-entered	1854	
†Henriette Boelow	1826	1827
Eliza Wilhelm. Vierling	1826	1829
Re-entered	1831	1832
Anna Abig. Leinbach	1826	1827
Re-entered town school	1829	1844
" academy	1844	1844
" town school	1845	
Anna Elizabeth Christ	1827	1839
Gertraut Spach	1827	1829
Lucia Theophila Benade	1827	1829
Sophia Dorothea Byhan	1827	1830
Doroth. Sophia Ruede	1827	1832
Re-entered	1834	1839
Lisette Schulz	1828	1839
M. Louisa Reich	1829	1836
†Lisette Meinung	1830	1836
Re-entered	1837	1844

		Entered.	Left.	Remarks.
59.	Martha Blum	1830	1832	Mrs. Griffin.
60.	Clara C. Reichel	1833	1834	
	Re-entered	1836	1841	Mrs. Hagen.
61.	Theresia Wilh. Bölow	1834	1840	Mrs. Siddal.
62.	†Maria Lavinia Blum	1835	1841	Died in the Academy.
63.	Dorothea Matilda Schulz	1835	1836	Mrs. Clewell.
64.	*Henriette Schnall*	1835		
65.	Louisa Hagen	1836	1839	Mrs. Susdorf.
66.	Henriette Shober	1837	1838	
67.	*Louisa Bülow*	1837		
68.	Louisa Rüde	1837	1840	Mrs. Rogers.
69.	Rahel Byhan	1838	1839	Mrs. Lineback.
70.	Theresa Petersen	1838	1843	
71.	Lucinda Pauline Blum	1839	1840	Mrs. Zevely.
72.	Henriette Reich	1839	1844	Mrs. Bölow.
73.	Melinda Senseman	1839	1847	Mrs. Hewitt.
74.	Susan Rights	1839	1842	
	Re-entered	1843	1846	Mrs. Keehln.
75.	Joh. Sophia Zevely	1839	1844	
	Re-entered	1845	1850	
	"	1851	1856	
76.	Anna Aurelia Herbst	1840	1841	Mrs. Reich.
77.	Miranda Rosalia Keehln	1840	1845	Mrs. Christ.
78.	†Louisa Lauretta Vogler	1841	1844	Mrs. Senseman.
79.	Sarah Ann Elvira Lineback	1841	1843	
	Re-entered	1844	1845	Mrs. Fulkerson.
80.	†Antoinette Bagge	1841	1842	Mrs. Brietz.
82.	†Henriette L. Petersen	1842	1843	Mrs. Friebele.
83.	Emma Aurelia Senseman	1842	1843	Mrs. Steward.
84.	Lucinda Bagge	1842	1843	
	Re-entered	1844	1844	
85.	*Lisette Brietz*	1843		
86.	Caroline M. Levering	1843	1845	Mrs. Rüde.
87.	Julia Blum	1843	1844	Mrs. Boner.
88.	Paulina E. Vogler, town school	1844	1844	
89.	Caroline B. Burkhard	1844	1845	Mrs. Rüde.
90.	Charlotte Smith	1844	1850	Mrs. Reinke.
91.	Angelica Reichel	1844	1849	
92.	Olivia S. Warner	1844	1844	
	Re-entered	1845	1849	
	"	1850	1851	
	"	1852	1856	
93.	*Emma Lineback*	1844	1852	
	Re-entered	1856		
94.	Augusta M. Hagen	1845	1847	
95.	Maria L. Hamen	1845	1848	Mrs. Christ.
96.	Francisca Benzien	1846	1848	
	Re-entered	1851	1854	Mrs. Fisher.
97.	Amelia C. Reichel	1847	1847	Mrs. Kummer.

SALEM FEMALE ACADEMY.—1804.

		Entered.	Left.	Remarks.
98.	Eliza Senseman	1847	1847	Mrs. Senseman.
	Re-entered	1855	1856	
99.	Augusta Hall	1847	1852	Mrs. Swink.
100.	Clementina Pfohl	1847	1849	Mrs. Meinung.
101.	Harriet Buttner	1847	1848	
102.	Sophia Foltz	1847	1855	
103.	*Ernestine T. Reichel*	1848		
104.	Elizabeth Haines	1848	1852	Mrs. Rights.
105.	†Ellen Wellfare	1848	1849	
106.	*Jane Wellfare*	1849		
107.	*Hermina Bensien*	1849		
108.	Emma Pfohl	1849	1851	Mrs. Grunert.
109.	*Louisa Herman*	1849	1851	
	Re-entered	1856		
110.	*Adelaide Herman*	1850		
111.	*Sophia Kremer*	1851	1853	
	Re-entered	1854		
112.	Emma Senseman	1851	1852	
113.	Adelaide Banner	1851	1852	Mrs. Everhart.
114.	Margaret Morrow	1852	1852	
115.	*Theophila Wellfare*	1852		
116.	Lisette Van Vleck	1852	1854	
117.	*Caroline Siewers*	1853		
118.	Ellen Blickensdörfer	1852	1855	Mrs. Starbuck.
119.	Louisa Van Vleck	1851	1851	
120.	*Maria Vogler*	1854		
121.	Anna Demuth	1855	1855	Mrs. Regenass.
122.	*Elizabeth Siewers*	1855		
123.	*Elizab. Chitty*	1856		
124.	*Gertrude Fant*	1856		

Of these 124 teachers, two have died in the Academy. Of the 3,470 scholars who entered the Institution, according to the following tables, only 12 have departed this life while at school.

In reference to the fourth column, showing the number at the close of the year, it is to be remarked that this is near the highest number of the year, as always more or less left the school at that time. The highest number of boarders, at one time in the house, was 230. The whole number of scholars during the year 1856, was 315, instructed by eighteen resident, and eleven non-resident teachers.

Statistical Table of Pupils in Salem Female Academy, from May, 1804, to Dec. 1856.

Years	No. entered during the year.	No. left during the year.	In school at the close of the year.	Virginia.	North Carolina.	South Carolina.	Georgia.	Alabama.	Mississippi.	Florida.	Louisiana.	Tennessee.	Kentucky.	Missouri.	Cherokee Nation.	Arkansas.	Indiana.	Ohio.	Texas.	Illinois.	California.
1804	10	6	10	3	10	5															
1805	37	40	41	5	27	18	1														
1806	39	36	40	4	19	8	2														
1807	37	30	41	6	22	10	1														
1808	27	30	38	1	13	7	1														
1809	29	38	37	18	9	18	2						1								
1810	51	51	50	8	19	11	8						4								
1811	73	42	72	10	22	20	3						5								
1812	63	62	83	18	28	9	11						7								
1813	65	58	86	5	18	10	8						4								
1814	57	43	85	15	12	22	6						9								
1815	55	56	98	7	9	17	7						6	1								
1816	54	65	98	6	13	14	12						6	1								
1817	71	45	103	4	21	18	4	1					12									
1818	60	69	116	9	23	21	3	1					14									
1819	56	47	83	8	10	10	9	1					3	1	1							
1820	66	47	104	11	29	15	6	6					6	1	1							
1821	49	51	102	7	17	9	10						7	1								
1822	53	41	113	10	11	16	7						5									
1823	73	61	125	16	23	27	7						7									
1824	65	79	101	12	17	18	6	6	1				7									

SALEM FEMALE ACADEMY.—1804.

XIII.

INDIAN MISSION.—1801.

From the very commencement of the settlement of the Moravian Brethren in North Carolina, it was their desire to resume the missionary labors among the Indian tribes of the South, for which in 1734 the first, though unsuccessful, attempts had been made in Georgia. During the Indian wars, when detached companies of Cherokee warriors enjoyed the hospitality of the "Dutch Fort," several chiefs expressed a desire of receiving teachers from the Moravians. Among the latter, Br. Ettwein especially took a deep interest in the spiritual welfare of these wild sons of the forest; and when taking his daily ride from Bethabara to Bethania, fraught with peril for life and limb, he in his silent meditations and communions with his Heavenly Master dedicated himself anew to His service, wherever it might be; and would have felt quite resigned to the will of the Lord, if through his being taken prisoner by the Indians he could have been enabled to proclaim to them the glad tidings of salvation. Nothing, however, could be done at that time. In 1775, a Cherokee chief, passing through Salem, assured the Brethren that they would be welcome amongst his nation, if they would instruct their children. After the close of the war, in 1784, Br. Martin Schneider paid a visit to the towns of the Cherokees on the Tennessee River. War, however, breaking out again soon after, for fifteen years nothing was heard directly from the Indians.

Meanwhile, a missionary society had been formed in Bethlehem in 1787, for propagating the Gospel among the heathen, and more especially the Indians of this continent. This society was joined by many Brethren in Salem, and thus the missionary spirit kept alive and fostered for more favorable times.[1]

[1] In the shady grove of the Bethabara graveyard is to be found the grave of one of the first missionaries

In October, 1799, at a meeting of the members of this society, several Brethren, and among them especially Br. Abraham Steiner, spoke very warmly for the so long neglected Indians. It was thereupon determined to visit them again, and the Brethren Abraham Steiner and F. C. de Schweinitz went in November to Tillico, a military station on the Tennessee, to have a talk with their red brethren in that vicinity. This visit was repeated in August, 1800, and, after many difficulties, the chiefs of the Cherokees gave a formal consent to the establishment of a school and mission station.

In 1801 this mission was commenced by Br. A. Steiner, assisted by G. Byhan, who, settling

of the Brethren's church, *Matthew Stack*, who had gone to Greenland in 1733, and commenced the mission there. He came to Bethabara in 1772, spending there in retirement his last years. January 19th, 1783, he was invited to Salem, to participate in the semi-centenary jubilee celebration of the Greenland mission, and in the love-feast gave an animated account of his experiences and trials in the missionary service. He died in 1787.

in July at a place called "The Springs," named this first missionary station *Springplace*. In 1802, Br. Steiner was succeeded by Br. Jacob Wohlfahrt as missionary, who remained till 1805, Br. Byhan serving as assistant till 1812.

In 1805, Br. *John Gambold* entered the Cherokee country as missionary, and served there with great fidelity for twenty-two years, closing his labors in *Oo-yu-ge-lo-gee*, the second mission station, commenced in 1821, where he departed this life, January 20th, 1827. His first wife, Anna Rosina Kliest (who died in 1821), had been sixteen years teacher in the Female Academy at Bethlehem, and was a very efficient help in the missionary labors of Br. Gambold. When they came to the Cherokee country (within the borders of Georgia, North Carolina and Tennessee), they found the prospects not very encouraging. The Cherokees, though taking the first steps towards civilization, seemed utterly averse to accepting the Gospel message; and though they could not but esteem the white stranger and his devoted wife, yet five years more elapsed until the widowed Cherokee Sister,

Margaret Vann, on August 13th, 1810, by holy baptism, was received into the communion of the Christian church, as the first visible fruit of nearly ten years' anxiety and toil. She was followed, in 1813, by Charles Hicks (by his baptismal name called Renatus), a man of influence among his nation. Gradually the number of believers increased, and in 1819 a meeting-house was built in Springplace.

In 1830 there were thirty-one baptized Indians belonging to the congregation of Springplace, and twenty at Ooyugelogee. At the former place Br. G. Byhan was stationed; at the latter, Br. H. G. Clauder. Both, however, were obliged soon after to leave the country, as they would not take the part of the Georgians against the Cherokees. Springplace and Ooyugelogee were abandoned in 1838. The Cherokee nation, and, with them, the Christian Indians, were compelled to emigrate. The Brethren J. R. Smith (who had served as missionary), Miles Vogler, and Herman Rüde accompanied them westward. On September 16th, 1838, the Mississippi River was reached, and there, in a solemn manner, the teachers of their flock closed with prayer their labors this side of the Father of Rivers. In the far West, in Arkansas Territory, the scattered remains of this mission were gradually collected again, and *New Springplace* and *Canaan* are the places where the mission work of the Moravians among the Cherokees is continued to this day.

The following Brethren have served successively as missionaries among the Cherokees:—

Abraham Steiner, 1801.

Gottl. Byhan, 1801—1812; 1827—1832.

Jacob Wohlfahrt, 1802—1805.

John Gambold, 1825—1827; 1827.

John Ren. Schmidt, 1820—1828; 1838—1839.

George Proske, 1822—1826.

Francis Eder, 1828—1829.

H. G. Clauder, 1828—1837.

Miles Vogler, 1837—1844; 1852—'54; 1854.

Gilbert Bishop, 1841.

D. Z. Smith, 1841—1849.

Edward Mock, 1847.

Alanson Wellfare, 1847—1855.

Samuel Warner.

In 1807 an attempt was made to carry the Gospel to the *Creek* nation, the Brethren Petersen and Burkhardt having been sent from Europe for this purpose. They, however, met with many obstacles, and some severe trials, amidst which Col. Hawkins, then the government agent, showed them much friendly aid. Suffering severely from fever, they were visited in 1810 by two Brethren from Salem, one of them, Dr. Shuman, affording them medical aid. Though the Indians along the Flint River received them kindly, still the main object of their mission was not attained; and the breaking out of the war obliged them to return to Salem, without having seen any fruit of their spiritual labor. Br. C. Petersen is still living in Salem, well stricken in years.

XIV.

NEGRO MISSION.—1822.

In February, 1822, a missionary society was organized among the Sisters of the Salem congregation, called "The Salem Female Missionary Society," for the purpose of aiding the missions of the United Brethren, and also to provide for the spiritual instruction of the Africans among and around us. The first officers of this Society were:—

Mrs. Susannah Elizab. Kramsch, *President*.
Sister Mary Steiner, *Treasurer*.
" Louisa E. Kramsch, *Secretary*.
" Susan E. Peter, *Collector*.
" Hedwig E. Shober, "
" Rebecca Holder, "
" Sarah Steiner, "

The formation of this society led to a resolution on the part of the Provincial Board to institute regular preaching for the colored people in and around Salem, and to form from amongst them a separate congregation. Br. Abr. Steiner kept the first service on March 24th, attended by about sixty hearers; ten of these formed the nucleus of the new congregation. Among these were four communicants. In 1823, a separate place of worship for the negroes was built near the old parish burial ground, and solemnly consecrated on the 28th of December. Here, all people of color have an opportunity of regularly hearing the preaching of the Gospel on the Lord's day; and the sacraments are also administered from time to time.

From the "Church Book for the people of color, in and about Salem, commenced 24th March, 1822, as the day on which it was first essayed to form them into a separate Christian Church," we have gleaned the following statistics:—

From 1822—1856, 174 children have been baptized, and 14 adults; 79 persons were buried, among these, 3 negroes above 80, 2 above 90, and 1 above 100 years of age; 10 marriages took place with the consent of the owners. The present number of communicant-members is 15. The following brethren have had the pastoral charge of this small congregation :—

    Brother Abr. Steiner, 1822—1832.
       "   J. R. Smith, 1832—1838.
       "   S. Th. Pfohl, 1838—1841.
       "   G. Byhan,   1842—1852.
       "   J. A. Friebele, 1853.

In December, 1847, Br. Jacob F. Siewers, of the Salem congregation, accompanied by his wife, set out on a new field of labor which seemed to open in East Florida at Mr. Alberti's plantation on the St. Mary's River, called *Woodstock Mills*. Though received with great kindness and liberality, supported by Mr. Alberti, still he soon found his position a very trying one, and that freedom of action was impeded by many obstacles. Not able to overcome these, he left in the fall of 1850, and Br. J. A. Friebele, who, at Mr. Alberti's urgent desire, had been sent there in 1851, also returned after remaining not quite two years.

XV.

HOME MISSION.—1835.

WOULD to God that all the Lord's people were prophets, and that the Lord would put his Spirit upon them! (Numb. xi. 29), was the answer of Moses, the man of God, when his servant Joshua in a complaining spirit told him that Eldad and Medad were prophesying in the camp. The Spirit of God had come upon them and they could not and would not resist. In a similar manner the Spirit of God came upon one of the working-men of Salem, a cabinet-maker by trade, who, in 1798, had assisted in the building of the Salem church. He felt an irresistible desire to go out of the camp, to seek the destitute and neglected, to go to the haunts of the intemperate and profane, to visit the hovels and cabins of those for whose souls' salvation no one seemed to care. A more destitute and forsaken region could hardly be imagined than was to be found in the Blue Ridge on the northern border of our State, twenty-five years ago. Drunkenness and gambling, sabbath-breaking and swearing, ignorance and vice reigned there supreme. No church, no schoolhouse was to be found far or near. Thither, following the divine impulse, and trusting to the guiding care of his Lord and Master—but still, with fear and trembling, Br. Van N. Zevely bent his steps in 1839. He was received with open arms by some, but on the majority his simple Gospel message seemed to make no impression; he was ridiculed and hooted at by the ignorant and vicious, and if he had gone to seek his own glory, he would have never gone again. But his heavenly Master had sent him, and in his own time he opened the hearts of those so long neglected mountaineers, and gradually the object of his visit was understood and appreciated.

Meanwhile, these missionary visits were exerting a silent but steady influence at home. A number of brethren and sisters, already inclined to do something in the cause of the Lord, readily responded to the call of forming a *Home Missionary Society*, and on Nov. 11th, 1835, this society was organized by the adoption of a constitution, of which the following is the preamble:—

"Whereas we, as members of the *Unitas Fratrum*, or Church of the United Brethren, in conformity with the spirit and purposes of our brethren, generally, throughout the world, feel it both as a duty and a warm desire of our hearts, to exert ourselves in promoting the spread of the saving knowledge of our Lord and Saviour Jesus Christ amongst our fellow-men, especially in such places as appear to be more destitute of Christian instruction than others; and

"Whereas, we feel ourselves encouraged by the abundant success which has crowned the endeavors of our brethren in other parts of the world, in attempting to benefit our Christian fellow-sinners, by sending unto them devoted and experienced men, in order to instruct and exhort, advise, and direct them; that, by the instrumentality of such friendly messengers of salvation, under the blessing of God, the ignorant may be taught, the careless roused, inquirers directed, the wavering established and strengthened, the thriving encouraged and confirmed; and all this in the simplest, plainest, most unobtrusive, but, at the same time, most affectionate and fervent manner—in imitation of Him, who went about doing good, and seeking to save that which is lost;

"Therefore, we the subscribers have resolved, in the name of God, to form ourselves for the attainment of the above-mentioned words, into a Society, under the name of the 'United Brethren's Home Missionary Society of North Carolina.'"

This society, numbers at present about 200 members.

At the first meeting of the Board, of which Bishop Bechler was President, Br. Zevely was regularly commissioned as Home Missionary of this society both for the mountain region of Virginia and some counties of North Carolina, south of Salem. He continued his visits from year to year. Especially along the road to the Volunteer Gap, a work of God became manifest.

A meeting-house was erected by the mountaineers, which, though destitute of architectural beauty, still answered all the purposes intended, and showed their willingness to receive the message of the Gospel. A number even applied for closer church-fellowship in 1838, which, however, was denied at the time, the German Diaspora[1] ideas still prevailing, and the consequence was, that others reaped where the Moravians had sown.

Meanwhile, Br. Zevely continued his labors, partly alone, partly in company of other Brethren, among which we name Br. John Vogler, and persevered, amidst no small occasional obstacles, until the infirmities of advanced age admonished him to intrust the main burden of the work to younger shoulders. Still, he continued to visit his children from time to time till 1856, when he, nearly seventy-six years old, bade them

---

[1] In Germany, the Diaspora laborers visit numbers of the established churches, not to proselytize, but to evangelize. In the United States, one cannot be separated from the other.

an affectionate adieu. About this time there were several of the families heretofore visited by Br. Zevely who desired to have their children baptized. As Br. Zevely was not an ordained minister, Bishop W. H. Van Vleck, at his solicitation, visited the mountain field, accompanied and conveyed thither by the before-mentioned Br. John Vogler. These three Brethren spent several weeks in the mountain trip, Br. Van Vleck preaching and baptizing, and all exhorting, encouraging, distributing religious tracts, &c. They were everywhere kindly received, even roads were especially opened for their carriage to pass, and many precious meetings held, to the edification of both parties.

Since 1845, the Brethren Rights, Rüde, and Hagen successively attended to this work, preaching partly in meeting-houses, partly in private dwellings, and also administering the holy sacraments to such as had become members of the church by baptism or confirmation.

It now became desirable to have a permanent station, where regular service might be held, and the holy sacraments be administered. After several attempts, a suitable locality, on "Ward's Gap," about nine miles north of Mt. Airy (fifty miles from Salem), was found; and, by the kind aid from Salem and the neighborhood of the place, means were raised for building a convenient church, which was solemnly consecrated to the Lord, by Bishop Herman, on November 24th and 25th, 1852. On the second day the members of the congregation now formed at this station, called *Mount Bethel*, partook, for the first time in the new church, of the holy communion.

In the spring of 1854, the missionary, Br. Jacob Siewers, removed to this station with his family, and found a temporary dwelling in the church, until, in June, 1855, the log house at the foot of the hill was so far completed that it could be occupied. Since then, a Sunday-school has been opened, and there is reason to hope that this work of the Lord will bear blessed fruits for eternity. The number of members at the close of 1856 was thirty-seven, of which twenty-seven are communicants.

XVI.

NEW CONGREGATIONS.—1830.

PREVIOUS to 1830, the "Western fever" had spread among many of the settlers on the Wachovia tract. Hearing of the rich soil of the far West, and looking upon their own poor, worn-out fields, and the innumerable gullies, washed out by the rains, gradually overspreading the arable land, many desired to better their temporal condition, and, forgetting for a while the higher wants of the soul, sold their plantations, and bent their steps to the untrodden wilderness of the far West. Thus especially the congregations of Hope and Friedland were considerably reduced in number. Among the wanderers was Br. *Martin Hauser*, a descendant of the first settlers of Bethania, hence often called Hausertown. After five weeks' toilsome journey, he reached Bartholomew County, in Indiana, in 1829, and found there some of his former neighbors, who, settling near each other, naturally desired to hear the preaching of the Gospel again, now more valuable to them than formerly, when within the sound of a church-bell. After some correspondence with the Provincial Helpers' Conference at Salem, Br. Hauser was appointed to hold meetings for the settlers. In 1830 a tract of two hundred and forty acres was bought, and the town *Hope* laid out. Br. L. D. de Schweinitz, then living at Bethlehem, visited the settlers in the same year, and on June 17th organized them into a Moravian congregation. In 1832 they were cheered by a visit of Br. Bechler, from Salem, and in 1838 the church erected there was solemnly consecrated by Bishop A. Benade, the President of the Northern Conference, and this congregation has ever since remained in connection with the northern section of the American Brethren's Church.

A similar settlement was commenced, about ten years later, in Edwards County, Illinois, whither some families from this neighborhood had emigrated. A year after its commencement, in 1846, Br. M. Hauser took charge of the gradually increasing congregation, as their minister; the place being now constituted as a separate Moravian congregation, by the name of *New Salem*, which, however, has since then been changed into *West Salem*, there being another New Salem in that State. In 1849 this congregation gained considerable accessions in numbers by a company of emigrants, who, having been in connection with the church in Germany, sought and found a welcome reception among their Brethren in this country.

This congregation, since 1851 under the pastoral care of Br. E. T. Senseman, remained in connection with the North Carolina section of the church till 1855, when, with the consent of all parties, it was transferred to the charge of the Northern Conference, and, with it, the home missionary work at Olney and other places.

Some members of the Bethania and other congregations had settled, twelve or fifteen years ago, and some even longer, in the neighborhood of a school-house six miles west of Salem. Different Brethren kept occasional services there until 1846, when a separate congregation was organized, called *New Philadelphia*, under the pastoral charge of Br. S. R. Hübner, of Salem. After the call of Br. Oerter to Bethabara, the care of this little flock devolved upon him for some time. Subsequently, steps were taken to erect a separate place of worship, with a burial-ground attached to it; and a convenient frame building was constructed during the year 1851. On the 31st of October and 1st of November of the same year, this building was solemnly dedicated as a house of God. Br. Siewers, after his return from Florida, served as pastor of this congregation until he removed to Mt. Bethel. Br. Rights, of Friedland, then attended to the spiritual wants of this small flock till the fall of 1854, since which time several Brethren at Salem have been preaching there at stated times, and administering the holy sacraments.

Within the last few years two new stations have been commenced by the pastor of the Friedberg congregation, at *Muddy Creek* and *Macedonia*. The former is situated west of

Friedberg, two or three miles on this side of the Yadkin River, and the latter in Davis County, the same distance on the other side, having received its name from the circumstance that a Macedonian cry came thence to the minister at Friedberg: Come *over* and help us. This cry was responded to by Br. Hagen, and his successor continues the work commenced by him at both places. At the old school-house, Muddy Creek, a congregation was organized in 1853, with seventeen communicant members, and in 1856 fifteen communicants were added to the Brethren's church at Macedonia, after the newly-erected log meeting-house had been solemnly dedicated to the service of the Triune God on May 25th and 26th of the same year.

XVII.

THE OLDER CONGREGATIONS.
1806—1856.

Concerning these last fifty years not much need be said, as many of the older members of the different congregations well remember the transactions in which they took part. But as dates are easily forgotten or misplaced, we add a short sketch.

In 1806 and 1807 a visit on the part of the Unity's Elders' Conference in Germany took place in our congregations, the Brethren J. R. Verbeek and Charles de Forestier, members of that Board, accompanied by their wives, having arrived for that purpose. These were present at the anniversary celebration of the congregation at *Bethabara*, November 17th, 1806, on which occasion a memorial-stone was placed, with solemn ceremonies, on the spot where the first twelve Brethren had found the cabin which afforded them shelter on their arrival. The inscription, "Wachovia settlement, begun 17th November, 1753," was cut upon this stone, which has since then been set up at the southeast corner of the Bethabara church.

In October of the same year, the corner-stone was laid for a new church at *Bethania*, and the building advanced, under the blessing of God, in the course of the two following years, so that the solemn consecration of it could take place on the 19th of March, 1809; the following day (20th) being set apart for the celebration of a semi-centenary jubilee in memory of the commencement of this congregation fifty years ago. Many Brethren and Sisters from the other congregations, as well as many persons from the neighborhood, shared in the solemnities of these days, which were principally conducted by Bishop Reichel, from Salem. It is worthy of remark, that of the original settlers six were present: Henry and Barbara Shorr, G. Michael and Elizabeth Ranke, and John and Catharine Beroth.

For several years, Brethren from Salem had preached occasionally in Germantown and Lexington, in the German and English languages, as also in Surrey County, in a Baptist church. In 1810, Br. Gottlieb Shober, since 1770 a member of the congregation at Salem, formally entered into the service of the Lutheran Church, as ordained pastor of several Lutheran congregations in the vicinity, and, for a time, also as president of the Lutheran Synod of North Carolina, still retaining his membership as a communicant of the Moravian Church.

In 1811, Bishop Loskiel, in Bethlehem, having been recalled to Europe, Bishop C. G. Reichel, of Salem, was appointed his successor by the Supreme Board of the Unity, and Br. *John Herbst*, of Litiz, Pa., received the pastoral charge of the Salem congregation. Having been ordained a bishop of the Brethren's church, he arrived in Salem in June, 1811; but in January, 1812, he was called home by his Heavenly Master, in the seventy-sixth year of his age. Though his ministration had been short, the sermons of the venerable bishop made a lasting impression on many. Br. Benzien had departed this life the November preceding, so that for a while Br. Simon Peter attended to the spiritual concerns of the Salem congregation.

In the fall of 1812 the vacancies were filled again, Br. *Jacob Van Vleck*, from Bethlehem, entering as president of the Provincial Board and pastor of the Salem congregation, and Br. L. D. de Schweinitz, who had resided some years in Germany, took the management of the financial affairs of the *province*. In 1815, Br. Van Vleck was ordained a bishop of the Brethren's church by Bishop Reichel.

In 1816 the congregation in Salem celebrated the semi-centenary jubilee of the commencement of this congregation, which at that time counted 374 members.

Towards the end of 1817, and more especially in the course of 1818, our settlements were visited by fevers, Salem and those south of it suffering most; in the former place, those attacked by the disease amounted to 160, several of whom on this occasion finished their course through time. This was also the case in Friedland, whereas Bethabara and Bethania continued almost free from the epidemic.

In 1822, Bishop Van Vleck resigned his offices, and retired from active service, and Br. *A. Benade*,[1] of Litiz, was appointed his successor, and consecrated a bishop of the Brethren's church. A boarding-school for boys was commenced at Salem in 1826, the former single Brethren's house being used for that purpose, but, however, for want of scholars, it was maintained less than two years.

On June 21st, 1828, the *Stokes County Sunday-School Union* was organized in Salem, under the presidency of Pastor Shober, and established Sunday-schools at Brushy Fork, Pleasant Hill, and elsewhere, which were numerously attended. In the following year, on March 29th, a great Sunday-school celebration took place in Salem, about six hundred children having assembled there from the neighborhood, with their teachers. The church being too small for the assembled

---

[1] Bishop Benade still resides at Bethlehem, aged nearly ninety.

multitude, the love-feast, prepared for the children, was held in the square. Since then, an annual sermon has been preached in reference to the Sunday-school cause, either in Salem or in one of the other congregations.

About the same time, the *Salem Tract Society* was formed, auxiliary to the American Tract Society. In 1829, also, the first sermon was preached in Salem in the *temperance* cause, and ten years later the *Stokes County Bible Society* was organized.

Bishop Benade having returned to Pennsylvania in 1828, was succeeded by Br. *J. C. Beckler*, from Litiz, as president of the Provincial Board. After the death of Br. G. B. Reichel, the pastor of the congregation, in 1834, Br. Beckler also served as minister of Salem. In 1835 he was ordained a bishop of the Brethren's church, and, as such, attended the General Synod of the church, held in Herrnhut, Germany, in 1836.

In the fall of 1836, Bishop *W. H. Van Vleck* entered here as president of the Wachovia Provincial Helpers' Conference, and pastor of the Salem congregation, faithfully discharging his manifold duties until failing strength compelled him to apply for assistants. During his term, a pulpit was erected in the Salem church in 1838, and used for the first time on Palm-Sunday; and in 1841, December 12th, the new chapel was consecrated, the last meeting in the old "congregation-house" having been held on December 9th. The *Young Men's Missionary Society* was also organized in that year.

The year 1843 was remarkable on account of the many cases of sickness. In the spring, 114 children in Salem (including about 70 boarders in the Female Academy) lay ill of the measles. In the fall, about 100 persons suffered from intermittent fevers; in the Friedberg neighborhood, about 350 cases of this sickness were counted; and afterwards the influenza prevailed to a considerable extent. Twenty-four funerals took place in Salem in that year.

After the General Synod of 1848, which Br. Van Vleck had attended, infirm health compelled him to resign his offices. They were divided between Bishop *J. G. Herman*, from Germany, and Br. *G. F. Bahnson*, from Lancaster, both entering in 1849, the former as president of the Provincial Board, the latter as pastor of the Salem congregation.

In the year 1849 important changes were commenced in the outward concerns of the Salem congregation. By a resolution of the Congregation Council, the monopolies existing hitherto were abolished, and free trade established. In the same year, the division of Stokes County was resolved upon by the inhabitants of the county, and, with the permission of the church authorities, fifty-one acres of Moravian lands were sold to the new county of *Forsythe*, and the new county-town of *Winston* took in a few years the place of the woods north of Salem, and the latter increased rapidly, till the boundary-line of Winston was reached.

In the course of time it became more and more evident that the former so-called "lease system" could not be longer maintained, according to which only members of the Moravian Church could be holders of real estate in the town of Salem, and, after mature deliberation, it was abolished on November 17th, 1856. By legislative enactment, soon after, a charter was obtained for the now incorporated borough of Salem, by which it has, outwardly, fully entered the ranks of other American towns, without, however, changing in the least the ecclesiastical connections of the congregation.

In 1853, on November 17th, the *Centenary Jubilee* of the Wachovia congregations was celebrated at *Bethabara*. Many Brethren and Sisters from the congregations of Salem, Bethania, Friedberg, Friedland, Hope, and Philadelphia having assembled, as well as a large number of friends and neighbors, the services of the day had to be conducted in the open air, for which the weather proved very favorable. In the evening a large number of persons marched, in solemn procession, by torchlight, preceded by the choir of trombones, up the adjacent hill, to the *burial-ground*, around which one hundred torches had been placed, which, surrounded by the forest-trees, afforded an impressive view. Here, in the stillness of a calm night, solemn hymns were sung, expressive of the happiness to be at home with the Lord, and in remembrance of those who, within the century past, had fallen asleep in Jesus, and whose mortal remains were here deposited; after which, all returned to the church, where, as the closing solemnity of the day, prayers were offered up and praise rendered once more unto Him whose mercies had been unfailing during the century past.

On the second day of this jubilee, besides other meetings, a solemn love-feast was kept in which about 1200 persons participated.

In 1854, soon after Easter, Bishop Herman left his home and family in Salem to make an official visitation to our mission among the Cherokee Indians in the Indian Territory. Having accomplished the object of his mission, he had gone several days on his homeward way when he was arrested by the hand of the Lord. A malignant fever, after a few days' illness, terminated his pilgrimage here below, and his services in the church militant. He departed this life on the 20th of July, about 1100 miles from his home, in Greene County, State of Missouri, in the 66th year of his age.

In December of the same year, his office, as

President of the Provincial Board, was filled again by the writer of this historical sketch, *Levin T. Reichel*, formerly stationed as pastor in Litiz, Pa.

SUMMARY AT THE CLOSE OF 1856.

		Communicants.	Non-communicants.	Children.	Total.
1.	Salem	430	59	209	698
2.	Bethabara	36	32	31	99
3.	Bethania	137	62	108	307
4.	Friedberg	164	114	151	429
5.	Muddy Creek	23	2	9	34
6.	Macedonia	15			15
7.	Hope	33	10	18	61
8.	Friedland	47	58	66	171
9.	Philadelphia	17	8	24	49
		902	345	616	1863

XVIII.

MINISTERS AND OTHER BRETHREN IN THE SERVICE OF THE PROVINCE IN GENERAL, AND OF THE SALEM CONGREGATION IN PARTICULAR.

1. DURING THE TIME OF THE BETHABARA ECONOMY.

		From	To	
1.	Bernh. A. Grube	1753	1754	
2.	Jacob Loesh, superintendent of plantations	1753	1769	
3.	John Jacob Fries	1754	1755	
4.	Gottlob Hoffman	1755	1764	
5.	Christ. H. Rauch	1755	1756	
6.	David Bishop	1756	1760	
7.	Christian Seidel, German minister	1756	1759	Died in office.
8.	J. M. Santer	1757	1760	Died in office.
9.	Jacob Rogers, English minister of Dobbs' Parish	1758	1762	
10.	John Ettwein, German minister	1759	1766	
11.	John Mich. Graff	1762	1773	
12.	Abrah. de Gammern	1762	1765	Died in office.
13.	Lawrence Bagge	1764	1769	
14.	Matthew Schropp	1766	1767	Died in office.
15.	Richard Utley, English minister of Dobbs' Parish	1766	1770	
16.	F. W. de Marshall			

2. BISHOPS AND MEMBERS OF THE PROVINCIAL HELPERS CONFERENCE.
(The Provincial Board. Nearly all living in Salem.)

		From	To	
1.	*Fred. Will. de Marshall*, S. C. President	1772	1802	Died in office.
2.	*John M. Graff*, Bishop, 1773	1772	1782	Died in office.
3.	Paul Tiersch	1772	1774	Died in office.
4.	Rich. Utley	1772	1775	Died in office.
5.	*John Daniel Koehler*, Bishop, 1790	1785	1800	
6.	Gottfried Praezel	1785	1788	Died in office.
7.	Christ. Lewis Benzien	1785	1811	Died in office.
8.	*Charles G. Reichel*, Bishop, President	1802	1811	
9.	Simon Peter, Bethabara	1803	1819	Died in office.
10.	*John Herbst*, Bishop, President	1811	1812	Died in office.
11.	Lewis D. de Schweinitz	1812	1821	
12.	*Jacob Van Vleck*, President, Bishop in 1815	1812	1822	
13.	Christ. Fr. Schaaf	1819	1841	Died in office.
14.	Theodor Shultz	1821	1849	
15.	*Andr. Benade*, Bishop, President	1822	1829	
16.	*John C. Beckler*, President, Bishop in 1835	1829	1836	
17.	*Will. H. Van Vleck*, Bishop, President	1836	1849	
18.	John C. Jacobson	1841	1844	
19.	Charles F. Kluge	1844	1853	
20.	*John G. Herman*, Bishop, President	1849	1854	Died in office.
21.	George F. Balmson	1849		
22.	Emil. A. de Schweinitz	1853		
23.	*Lewis T. Reichel*, President	1854		

3. MINISTERS OF SALEM.

		From	To	
1.	Paul Fiersch	1771	1774	Died in office.
2.	John M. Graff, Epis.	1774	1782	Died in office.
3.	John Fr. Peter	1782	1784	
4.	John Dan. Koehler, Epis.	1784	1800	
5.	Chr. Benzien	1800	1802	
6.	Charles G. Reichel, Epis.	1802	1811	
7.	John Herbst, Epis.	1811	1812	Died in office.
8.	Simon Peter	1812	1812	
9.	Jacob Van Vleck, Epis.	1812	1822	
	G. Benj. Reichel, assistant	1819	1829	
10.	Andr. Benade, Epis.	1822	1829	

MINISTERS OF SALEM—Continued.

		From	To	
11.	G. Benj. Reichel, minister	1829	1833	Died in office.
12.	John C. Beckler, Epis.	1833	1836	
14.	Will. H. Van Vleck, Epis.	1836	1849	
	Henry A. Shultz, assistant	1839	1842	
	Charles A. Bleck, "	1842	1844	
	Sam'l R. Huebner, "	1844	1849	Died in office.
	A. A. Reinke "	1848	1849	
15.	George F. Bahnson.	1849		

4. WARDENS OF SALEM CONGREGATION.

(Having the management of the outward affairs. Not all of them ordained brethren.)

1.	John Klein	1770	1770	Died in office.
2.	Richard Utley	1771	1774	
3.	J. G. Wallis	1774	1776	
4.	C. G. Reuter, surveyor	1776	1777	Died in office.
5.	J. H. Herbst	1778	1780	
6.	Jeppe Wiclsen (two weeks)	1780	1780	Died in office.
7.	G. Praezel	1781	1788	Died in office.
8.	J. H. Herbst	1788	1790	
9.	Abrh. Hessler	1790	1791	
10.	Samuel Stotz	1791	1820	Died in office.
	John Gambold, assistant	1802	1804	
	Mast. Schneider, "	1804	1806	
11.	G. Byhan	1820	1827	
12.	Will. L. Benzien	1827	1832	Died in office.
	Vacancy.			
13.	S. Thomas Pfohl	1837		

Besides these brethren (and the administrators and principals of Female Academy mentioned, ch. II. and XII.), there have been a number of Brethren, some of them ordained as Deacons of the Brethren's Church, who, from 1769 to 1823, attended more especially to the spiritual and temporal concerns of the single Brethren's establishment. In a similar manner Sisters have been in the service of the church as superintendents of the choir house of the single Sisters.

There were brethren, also, occasionally appointed as superintendents of the Salem boy-school, among whom we name, because he has not been mentioned elsewhere, C. Th. Pfohl, who served in that capacity from 1791 to 1802.

Since 1849, the boys' school has been placed under a committee consisting of the ministers and wardens of the congregation, and three brethren elected by the congregation council.

The number of scholars at the close of 1856 was fifty.

There is also, since 1836, an infant school established in the now so-called "Widows' House," managed by a Sister, averaging about thirty children.

XIX.

MINISTERS OF THE COUNTRY CONGREGATIONS.

(Only the resident ministers are mentioned in the following lists.)

1. BETHABARA.

		From	To	
1.	Lawrence Bagge	1773	1784	
2.	John Jacob Ernst	1784	1791	
3.	Abraham Hessler	1791	1800	Died in office.
4.	John Jacob Ernst	1800	1802	
5.	C. D. Buchholz. June to Oct.	1802	1802	
6.	Simon Peter	1802	1811	
7.	J. P. Kluge, assistant in 1807	1811	1813	
8.	J. L. Strohle	1813	1827	Died in office.
	Vacant.			
9.	G. Byhan	1832	1837	
	Vacant.			
10.	J. R. Schmidt	1839	1847	
	Vacant.			
11.	L. T. Oerter	1849	1854	
	Attended to by the minister of Bethania.			

2. BETHANIA.

		From	To	
1.	David Bishop	1760	1763	Died in office.
2.	L. G. Bachhof	1761	1770	
3.	John J. Ernst	1770	1784	
4.	Valentin Beck	1784	1791	Died in office.
5.	Simon Peter	1791	1802	
6.	Christ. Th. Pfohl	1802	1823	
7.	J. P. Kluge, assistant	1813	1819	
8.	Peter Wolle, "	1819	1822	
9.	Charles A. Van Vleck	1822	1826	
10.	J. C. Jacobson	1820	1834	
11.	G. F. Bahnson	1834	1838	
12.	Julius T. Beckler	1838	1844	
13.	F. F. Hagen	1844	1851	
14.	E. M. Grunert	1851		

For a time two ordained Brethren were stationed at Bethania, and Brother C. Lash had the management of the temporal affairs of the congregation, which was to be placed on the same footing as Salem, as a so-called "Place Congregation," with lease system, etc. The place was finally abandoned in 1822.

3. FRIEDBERG.

		From	To	
1.	L. G. Bachhoff	1770	1776	Died in office.
2.	Valent. Beck	1776	1784	
3.	Simon Peter	1784	1791	
4.	Martin Schneider	1791	1804	
5.	John Gambold	1804	1805	
6.	C. D. Buchholz	1805	1806	
7.	C. H. Rüde	1807	1822	
8.	C. F. Denke	1822	1832	
9.	H. A. Schultz	1832	1839	
10.	S. R. Hübner	1839	1844	
11.	E. T. Senseman	1844	1851	
12.	F. F. Hagen	1851	1854	
13.	Lewis Rights	1854		

4. HOPE.

		From	To	
1.	J. Chr. Fritz	1780	1787	
2.	J. Jac. Wohlfert	1787	1792	
3.	Samuel G. Kramsch	1792	1802	
4.	Abrah. Steiner	1802	1806	
5.	J. Jac. Wohlfert	1807	1807	Died in office.
6.	J. L. Strohle	1807	1813	
7.	Samuel G. Kramsch	1813	1819	
8.	C. F. Denke	1820	1821	
	The place was considered too unhealthy, and no minister resided there till 1838. In 1839 a new minister's house was built, but abandoned in 1841.			

MINISTERS OF COUNTRY CONGREGATIONS. 171

HOPE—*Continued.*

		From	To	
9.	H. G. Clauder	1838	1839	
10.	Adam Haman	1839	1841	
	This congregation is at present under the pastoral charge of the ministers at Friedberg.			

5. FRIEDLAND.

		From	To	
1.	Toege Nissen	1775	1780	
2.	John Casper Heinzman . .	1780	1783	Died in office.
3.	Peter Goetje	1783	1786	Died in office.
4.	J. Martin Schneider . .	1786	1791	
5.	J. J. Ernst	1791	1800	
6.	J. Jacob Wohlfert . . .	1801	1802	
7.	C. D. Buchholz . . .	1802	1805	
8.	J. J. Wohlfert	1805	1806	
9.	C. D. Buchholz . . .	1807	1823	
10.	S. R. Hübner	1823	1827	
11.	S. Thomas Pfohl . . .	1827	1837	
12.	G. Byhan	1837	1841	
13.	Adam Haman	1841	1843	
	Non-resident minister, attended by S. R. Hübner, from Salem.			
14.	Lewis Rights, assistant in 1846	1847	1851	
15.	F. F. Hagen	1351	1851	
16.	Lewis Rights	1851	1854	
	Vacant.			
17.	J. C. Cooke	1856		

XX.

THE BRETHREN'S UNITY.

BEFORE closing this historical sketch, it will be necessary to make a few remarks in reference to the ecclesiastical connection of the Wachovia Moravian Congregations with the other congregations of the Brethren's Unity. By capital from abroad the land was bought, the forests cleared; by emigrants and colonists from Europe and Pennsylvania the settlements were commenced, and though their descendants are now fully able, by native talent and their own resources, to maintain what their self-denying grandsires have established for them, still not only they are gratefully remembered by every upright Moravian, but the connection hitherto existing with the other parts of the *Unitas Fratrum*, is cheerfully maintained, with such modifications as altered circumstances necessarily require.

Whilst formerly official visitations on the part of the governing Board of the Unity were deemed indispensable to maintain the connection, in modern times this object has been gained by the occasional visit of Brethren from our parts as deputies to the General Synods, hitherto always held in Germany. These delegates were, on former occasions, elected or appointed by the Provincial Board or the Congregations of the Province. By the last General Synod of 1848, an alteration has been resolved upon, according to which two brethren, elected by the Province itself through its representation assembled at a Provincial Synod in 1856,[1] are to go to the General Synod of the Unity to be convened in Herrnhut, June 8th, of this year, with the following declaration:—

"Whereas, the Brethren's *Unity* is composed of very different parts, which, however, all be-

---

[1] *Vide* Digest of the Provincial Synod at Salem, held April 28th to May 13th, 1856.

long either to the Brethren's *Church* or to the Brethren's *Congregation;* and

"Whereas, we are, nevertheless, all built on the same foundation, that of the apostles and prophets, Jesus Christ himself being the chief corner-stone;

"Therefore *resolved*, that, though belonging to different nationalities, speaking different languages, living under different forms of government, cherishing different political views, and having different social habits, still a Bond of Union, connecting the different branches of the *Unitas Fratrum*, can be, and we hope and pray may be maintained also in future years, and we continue to be 'the *Brethren's Unity*, even without uniformity.'"

This union feeling has been strengthened and nourished by the celebration of our memorial days, both annually and centenary. Thus, in June, 1822, the several congregations of this province, in spiritual union with our other congregations in the four parts of the globe, celebrated the *Centenary Jubilee* of the *Renewed Church* of the Brethren; the 17th of June, 1722, being the day, from which dates the beginning of Herrnhut, the mother congregation of the renewed church. Ten years later, in 1732, a similar festive commemoration was held of the first attempt of the church in August, 1732, to go forth in the faith and strength of the Lord, to proclaim the glad tidings of salvation to the benighted heathen.

And being descendants of the old church of martyrs, which was established in the mountains of Bohemia in 1457, the oldest of the protestant churches, we this year celebrate, with fervent gratitude to the Lord, the *Fourth Centenary* of the *Unitas Fratrum*.

MARCH 1st, 1857.

APPENDIX.

APPENDIX No. I.

FIRST SETTLERS AND HEADS OF FAMILIES.

This list has been carefully extracted from the church records of the different Moravian congregations in North Carolina; and many of the present members of the church will, no doubt, be gratified to find on record here, when their ancestors arrived in this country, and where their burial places may be found.

ACKERMAN, John, born in 1756, near Eisenach, Germany; came to North Carolina in 1785; died in 1791 in Bethabara.

BAGGE, Traugott, born in 1729 in Gottenburg, Sweden; came to North Carolina in 1768; died in 1800 in Salem.

BAUMGARTEN, John George, born in 1722 in Hesse Cassel; came to North Carolina in 1755; died in 1779 in Salem.

BEROTH, Jacob, born in 1740 in York Co., Pa.; came to North Carolina in 1772; died in 1801 in Salem.

BEROTH, John, born in 1725 in Oppen. Palatinate, one

of the first settlers of Bethabara in 1753, and of Bethania in 1759; died in 1817 in Friedland.

BLUM, Jacob, born in 1739 in Saucon, Northampton, Pa.; came to North Carolina in 1768; died in 1802 in Salem.

BLUM, John Henry, born in 1752 in Bethlehem, Pa.; came to North Carolina in 1766; died in 1824 in Salem.

BOECKEL, John Nicolaus, born in 1741 in Heidelberg, Pa.; came to North Carolina in 1767; died in 1822 in Bethania.

BOECKEL, Fred., born in 1742 in Pennsylvania; came to North Carolina in 1765; died in 1802 in Friedberg.

BÖLOW (Belo), John Fred., born in 1780 in Herrnhut, Saxony; came to North Carolina in 1806; died in 1827 in Salem.

BONER, Joseph William, born in 1747 in Pennsylvania; came to North Carolina in 1769; died in 1785 in Hope.

BRIEZ, Christian, born in 1772 in Lower Lusatia, Germany; came to North Carolina in 1806; died in 1845 in Salem.

BURKHARDT, John Christian, born in 1771 in Tangermünde, Alt Mark, Prussia; came to North Carolina in 1806; died in 1846 in Salem.

APPENDIX. 181

BUTTNER, Thomas, born in 1741 in Monocasy, Maryland; came to North Carolina in 1768; died in 1780 in Hope.

BYHAN, Gottlieb, born in 1777 near Herrnhut, Saxony; came to North Carolina in 1796.

CHITTY, John, born in 1766 in Maryland; died in 1825 in Bethabara.

CHRIST, Rudolph, born in 1750 in Wurtemberg; came to North Carolina in 1765; died in 1833 in Salem.

CHRISTMAN, Balthasar, born in 1760 in York Co., Pa.; came to North Carolina in 1780; died in 1797 in Bethabara.

CLAUDER, Charles Gottlieb, born in 1765 in Zwickau, Saxony; came to North Carolina in 1797; died in 1843 in Salem.

CONRAD, Christian, born in 1744 in Pennsylvania; came to North Carolina in 1768; died in 1800 in Bethania.

COOK (Koch), George, born in 1771 in Lancaster, Pa.; came to North Carolina in 1806; died in 1822 in Friedberg.

DOUTHID, John, born in 1709 in Coleraine, Ireland; came to North Carolina in 1750; died in 1784 in Hope.

EBERHARDT, John Lewis, born in 1758 in Thuringia,

16

Germany; came to North Carolina in 1799; died in 1839 in Salem.

EBERT, John Martin, born in 1727 in Anspach, Germany; came to North Carolina in 1774; died in 1792 in Friedberg.

ELROD, Christian, born in 1721 in Pennsylvania; came to North Carolina in 1751; died in 1785 in Hope.

FETTER, Jacob, born in 1781 in Lancaster, Pa.; died in 1856 in Salem.

FISCHELL, John Adam, born in 1730 in Palatinate, Germany; came to North Carolina in 1779; died in 1802 in Friedberg.

FISHER, Melchior, born in 1726 in Heilbron, Wurtemberg; came to North Carolina about 1770; died in 1798 in Friedberg.

FOCKEL, Gottlieb, born in 1724 in Peilau, Silesia, Germany; came to North Carolina in 1755; died in 1778 in Bethabara.

FREY, Peter, born in 1689 in Alsace, Germany; came to North Carolina in 1765; died in 1766 in Friedberg.

FRIES, John Christ William, born in 1775 in Barby, Germany; came to North Carolina in 1809.

GRABS, Gottfried, born in 1716 in Silesia, Germany; came to North Carolina in 1756; died in 1793 in Bethania.

APPENDIX. 183

GREETER, Jacob, born in 1708 in Alsace, Germany; came to North Carolina in 1768; died in 1788 in Friedberg.

HAGEN, John Joachim, born in 1771 in Brandenburg; came to North Carolina in 1814; died in 1844 in Salem.

HANKE, John, born in 1750 in Nazareth, Pa.; died in 1823 in Bethania.

HAMILTON, Horatio, born in 1756 in Frederick Co., Maryland; came to North Carolina in 1775; died in 1840 in Hope.

HARTMAN, George Fred., born in 1724 in Palatinate; came to North Carolina in 1755; died in 1788 in Friedberg.

HAUSER, Martin, born in 1696 in Mümpolgard, Switzerland; came to North Carolina in 1753; died in 1761 in Bethania.

HEGE, John Balthasar, born in 1714 in Wurtemberg; came to North Carolina in 1757; died in 1785 in Bethania.

HEIN, John Jacob, born in 1713 in Dilleburg, Germany; died in 1795 in Friedland.

HEIN, John, born in 1749 near Dilleburg, Germany; died in 1806 in Bethabara.

HERBST, John Henry, born in 1727 in Hanover; came to North Carolina in 1762; died in 1821 in Salem.

HORN, Marcus, born in 1719 in Zweibrücken, Germany; came to North Carolina in 1774; died in 1797 in Friedberg.

HOLDER, George, born in 1729 in Oley, Pa.; came to North Carolina in 1755; died in 1804 in Bethabara.

HOLLAND, John, born in 1743 in Cheshire, England; came to North Carolina in 1773; died in 1811 in Salem.

KAPP, John Jacob, born in 1729 in Switzerland; came to North Carolina in 1754; died in 1807 in Bethabara.

KÖRNER, Joseph, born in 1769 in Black Forest, Germany; died in 1830 in Friedland.

KRAUSE, Matthew, born in 1720 in Upper Silesia, Germany; came to North Carolina in 1755; died in 1762 in Bethabara.

KRON, Peter, born in 1722 in Eichfeld, Franconia; died in 1798 in Friedland.

KEEHLN, Christian David, born in 1793 in Niesky, Germany; came to North Carolina in 1818.

KÜNZEL, John Fred., born in 1737 in Königsbach, Germany; died in 1802 in Friedland.

LAGENOUR, Jacob Fred., born in 1751 in Durlach, Germany; died in 1843 in Friedland.

LEHMAN, John Christian, born in 1770 in Lusatia, Germany.

APPENDIX.

LEINBACH, Lewis, born in 1743 in Oley, Pa.; came to North Carolina in 1765; died in 1800 in Bethabara.

LEINBACH, Frederick, born in 1737 in Oley, Pa.; died in 1821 in Salem.

LICK, Martin, born in 1726 in Neuwied, Germany; came to North Carolina in 1758; died in 1760 in Bethabara.

LOESH (Lash), John Jacob, born in 1722 in Schoharie, N. Y.; came to North Carolina in 1753; died in 1782 in Hope, N. J.

MACK, Jacob, born in 1753 in Reading, Pa.; died in 1836 in Davidson County.

MEINUNG, Charles Lewis, born in 1743 in Oley, Pa.; came to North Carolina in 1771; died in 1817 in Salem.

MÜCKE, John, born in 1749 near Philadelphia; died in 1807 in Bethabara.

MÜLLER; Jacob, born in 1721 in Zweibrücken, Germany; died in 1798 in Bethania.

MOSS, Henry, born in 1751 in Maryland; came to North Carolina in 1775; died in 1822 in Friedberg.

NOLL, Jacob, born in 1740 near Philadelphia; died in 1811 in Bethabara.

NÖTHING, Matthew, born in 1756 in Halifax; died in 1807 in Salem.

OEHMAN, John Gottfried, born in 1781 in Weissenstein, Livonia, Russia; came to North Carolina in 1819.

OPIZ, Charles, born in 1719 in Silesia, Germany; came to North Carolina in 1755; died in 1763 in Bethania.

PADGET, John, born in 1723 in Charles County, Maryland; came to North Carolina in 1775; died in 1811 in Hope.

PADGET, Thomas, born in 1752 in Carrol's Manor, Maryland; came to North Carolina in 1775; died in 1831.

PETERSEN, Carsten, born in 1776 near Flensburg, Denmark; came to North Carolina in 1806.

PEDDICOART, William Barton, born in 1739 in Prince George's County, Maryland; came to North Carolina in 1775; died in 1807 in Hope.

PFAFF, Peter, born in 1727 in Palatinate, Germany; came to North Carolina in 1771; died in 1804 in Bethania.

PHILIPPS, John Samuel, born in 1776 in Pennsylvania.

RANKE, John, born in 1737 in Lancaster County, Pa.; came to North Carolina in 1754; died in 1798 in Bethabara.

REICH, John Christoph, born in 1763 in Berks County, Pa.; died in 1824 in Salem.

APPENDIX. 187

Reich, Matthew, born in 1764 in Berks County, Pa.; died in 1829 in Salem.

Reich, Jacob, born in 1770 in Orange County, N. C.; died in 1827 in Friedberg.

Reuz (Rights), John, born in 1752 in Bethlehem, Pa.; came to North Carolina in 1764; died in 1810 in Salem.

Ried, Jacob, born in 1735 in Baden Durlach; came to North Carolina in 1770, from Broad Bay, Maine; died in 1819 in Friedland.

Rominger, David, born in 1716 in Wurtemberg; came to North Carolina, from Broad Bay, Maine, in 1769; died in 1777 in Bethabara.

Rominger, Michael, born in 1709 in Wurtemberg; came to North Carolina, from Broad Bay, in 1770; died in 1803 in Friedland.

Rothrock, Philip, born in 1746 in York County, Pa.; died in 1825 in Friedberg.

Rothrock, Peter, born in 1746 in York County, Pa.; died in 1829 in Friedberg.

Rothrock, Jacob, born in 1770 in York County, Pa.; died in 1807 in Friedberg.

Schaffner, John, born in 1773 in Switzerland; came to North Carolina in 1818; died in 1854 in Salem.

Schaub, John Fred., born in 1717 in Switzerland; came

to North Carolina in 1755; died in 1801 in Bethania.

SCHNEIDER, Melchior, born in 1717 in Durlach, Germany; came to North Carolina, from Broad Bay, Maine, in 1770; died in 1790 in Friedland.

SCHORR, Henry, born in 1735 in Switzerland; came to North Carolina in 1756; died in 1819 in Bethania.

SCHULZ, John, born in 1703 in Basle, Switzerland; came to North Carolina in 1769; died in 1788 in Bethania.

SCHUMAN, Fred. Henry, born in 1777 in Gnadau, Germany; came to North Carolina in 1808.

SEIZ, John Michael, born in 1737 in Wurtemberg; came to Broad Bay, Maine, in 1759, and to North Carolina in 1770; died in 1817 in Friedland.

SENSEMAN, John Henry, born in 1786 in Heidelberg, Pa.; died in 1854 in Salem.

SHOBER, Gottlieb, born in 1756 in Bethlehem, Pa.; came to North Carolina in 1768; died in 1838 in Salem.

SPACH, Adam, born in 1720 in Alsace, Germany; came to North Carolina in 1756; died in 1801 in Friedberg.

SPOENHAUER, John Henry, born in 1716 in Switzerland;

came to North Carolina in 1755; died in 1788 in Bethania.

STAUBER, Paul Christian, born in 1726 in Frankfurt, Germany; came to North Carolina in 1767; died in 1793 in Bethania.

STOCKBURGER, John George, born in 1731 in Wurtemberg; came to North Carolina in 1766; died in 1803 in Salem.

STOLZ, Caspar, born in 1753 in Pennsylvania; died in 1834 in Bethania.

STRUP, John Francis, born in 1716 in Nassau, Germany; came to North Carolina in 1766; died in 1782 in Bethabara.

STRUP, John, born in 1719 in Lauffelfingen, Germany; came to North Carolina in 1760; died in 1789 in Bethania.

TESCH, Henry, born in 1733 in Palatinate; came to North Carolina in 1771; died in 1804 in Friedberg.

TRANSON, Philip, born in 1724 in Palatinate; came to North Carolina in 1762; died in 1792 in Bethania.

VIERLING, Samuel Benjamin, born in 1765 in Rudolstadt, Silesia, Germany; came to North Carolina in 1790; died in 1817 in Salem.

VOGLER, Philip Christopher, born in 1725 in Palatinate;

came to North Carolina, from Broad Bay, Maine, in 1770; died in 1790 in Bethania.

VOLZ, Peter, born in 1726 in Alsace, Germany; came to North Carolina in 1768; died in 1806 in Friedberg.

WAGMAN, Andrew, born in 1758 in South Carolina; came to North Carolina in 1766; died in 1779 in Salem.

WERNER, Christian Andrew, born in 1768 in Randolph County, N. C.; died in 1814 in Bethania.

WESNER, Matthew, born in 1730 in Stuttgart, Wurtemberg; came to North Carolina in 1772; died in 1806 in Friedberg.

WINKLER, Christian, born in 1766 in Switzerland; came to North Carolina in 1807; died in 1839 in Salem.

ZEVELY, Van Naman, born in 1780 in North Carolina; came to Salem in 1798.

ZIMMERMAN, Christian, born in 1726 in Nassau, Germany; came to North Carolina in 1758; died in 1793 in Friedberg.

No. II.
CHURCHES AND OTHER PUBLIC BUILDINGS.

SALEM.

First meeting hall in Congregation House consecrated 13th Nov. 1771.

The house removed in 1854 to make room for the new academy building.

Church of Salem consecrated 9th Nov.	1800
Chapel built in	1841
Old academy finished	1805
Boys' school-house	1794
Single sister's house	1786
Brethren's house	1769

BETHABARA.

First meeting house, consecrated		1st Feb. 1756.
Present church,	"	26th Nov. 1788.

BETHANIA.

First meeting house,	"	23d June, 1771.
Present church	"	22d Oct. 1806.

FRIEDLAND.

First meeting house,	"	18th Feb. 1775.
Second " "	"	31st Oct. 1847.

FRIEDBERG.

First " "	"	11th March, 1769.
Second " "	"	12th March, 1788.
Third " "	"	28th July, 1827.

Hope meeting house, consecrated 28th March, 1780.
Philadelphia meeting house, " 31st Oct. 1851.
Macedonia " " " 25th May, 1856.

NEW ACADEMY BUILDINGS.

For future reference, we insert here a full description of the New Female Academy at Salem, which was prepared for the "*Moravian*," vol. i. 4, the official organ of the American Moravian Church.

"The new house occupies the site of the old church and parsonage (formerly called the 'Congregation House'), immediately joining the original school building.

"The dimensions of the *main building* are 100 feet front by 52 feet deep, with a wing at the north $70\frac{1}{2}$ feet in length and $34\frac{1}{2}$ feet in depth, and another one at the south 77 by 44 feet. The main building, as well as the north wing, is four stories on the front, and at the rear (on account of the descent of the ground) five stories, including the basement. The fronts of the houses are of pressed brick, expressly manufactured for our building, and are probably some of the first of the kind made in our State.

"The front is ornamented by a large *Doric portico*, 50 feet in length and 13 feet in width. It has four Doric columns, with two pilasters resting against the house. The height of the whole, including bases, columns, and entablatures, is between 30 and 40 feet—the cornice of the entablature extending three feet above the sills of the third story windows. The whole is built strictly in accordance with the classical Doric order of architecture. The columns are of brick, stuccoed with hydraulic cement in imitation of brown sandstone, as is also the rest of the portico, excepting the bases and steps, which are of hewn granite.

"The *roof* of the house has but one inclination, from front to rear, and is covered with tin. The front elevation is formed and crowned by a very heavy cornice of blockwork, over six feet in height. In the centre, there rises above this, a pediment of over fifty feet in length of base, by about eighteen feet elevation.

"The *first* and *second* stories of the main house are divided into eighteen dwelling and school rooms, with smaller side rooms attached to each. These side rooms are fitted up with small closets, wardrobes, &c. All the rooms are lined, to a height of three feet from the floor, with panel-work, grained in imitation of walnut. Passages of 12 feet wide extend through the whole length of the house in each story, and wide staircases run up on both ends of the main house, from the basement to the fourth story. The entrance-hall, on the first floor, into which the large front door opens, is about 20 feet square, connecting with the main passage by an elliptical archway of about 20 feet span. On the south end the passage connects by a closed and covered way with the old buildings.

"The whole *third* floor forms one dormitory. This is a very large room, extending over the entire house from wall to wall, without any partitions, the ceiling and fourth floor being supported by a colonnade of sixteen pillars.

"The *fourth* story is divided into ten rooms; those on the front being fine and airy, intended for smaller classes and music rooms. Those on the rear are roughly finished, and only intended for trunk and store rooms.

"The *north wing* is divided into a large number of rooms, to be used for various purposes. The whole of the second story of this wing is devoted to the so-called 'sick-rooms,' with every convenience attached. From this wing there is also a covered and closed way, leading directly into our church, and by this passage our scholars can enter the church under cover at all times.

"The whole rear part of the *basement* story is taken up by 'wash' or 'dressing-rooms.' There are eighteen such wash-rooms, each being furnished with three stationary basins. Through all these apartments the water, both hot and cold, is conducted in pipes, with cocks over each basin. In addition to these rooms there are a number of bath-rooms, with tub and shower baths. The head of water is obtained from large water

APPENDIX.

tanks, located in the building at the end of the north wing. The supply of water is procured from a well and spring at the foot of the hill upon which the building stands, being driven up to an elevation of some 140 feet by forcing-pumps, which are worked by water-power. The hot water is generated in a large circulating boiler, located in the cellar of the front house. This boiler was made expressly for our establishment in Auburn, New York.

"There are *porches* of 12 feet width, extending along the rear of the house, two stories high on the main house, and three on the north wing.

"We have introduced a very complete system of ventilation throughout the whole building. Four main trunk ventilators run up from the lower floor, extending above the roof. With these main trunks, the different rooms are connected by branches.

"The *south wing* is not yet quite completed. The lower floor of this wing will contain a dining-room, large enough to seat some 250 persons. On the second floor, which will be supported by iron pillars, our *chapel* will be located."

R. DE. S.

No. III.
HOUSES BUILT IN SALEM.
1766—1816.

1766. Feb., first house,   at present, Schaffner's shop.
Aug., second house,   owned by Fries.
" third house, two-story building, since removed,   site of Fries's store. Contained first meeting-hall.

1767. Fourth house,   inhabited by W. Leibech.
Fifth "   inhabited by Hughes.
Sixth "   owned by Ebert.

1768. Pottery,   inhabited by J. Chitty.
Blacksmith-shop,   at present, L. Belo.
Single Brethren's house.

1769. Single Brethren's house, finished in part,   at present, widows' house.
Tannery,   at present, Brietz.

1770. Congregation-house, finished in 1771, removed in 1854.
Seventh house,   at present, Fischer.

1771. House for skins,   at present, Belo's store.
Tavern, burnt in 1784, rebuilt in 1784,   at present, Buttner.

1772. Reuter's house,   " J. Vogler.

1774. Store of congregation,   " E. A. Vogler.
Triebel's house,   rebuilt in 1756, W. H. Hall.

APPENDIX.

1775. Family house.
1783. Family house, afterwards widows' house, since removed, at present, bank building.
1785. Single Sisters' house.
   Family house, at present, Shober's.
1786. Family house, formerly Huesler's.
   Addition to Brethren's house.
1787. Family house, at present, Thos. Boner.
   "   "   inhabited by Mitchel.
1788. "   "   "   " Banner.
1789. Fulling-mill, at present, N. Vogler.
1791. Family house, at present, Boner & Crist's store.
1794. Boys' school-house.
1797. House for warden of congregation, S. Stotz,
   at present, S. Th. Pfohl.
   C. Vogler's house,   "   R. Crist.
1800. Dr. Vierling's house,   "   land-office.
   Bakery,   "   Winkler.
1803. Girls' school-house.
   Market-house on the square.
   Corpse-house.
1805. Schröter's house, at present, Fulkerson.
1810. Inspector's house.
1814. Eberhardt's house.
   C. Schulz's   "   at present, Schaffner.
1815. Chr. Reich (copper-smith).

The above list is not quite complete, for in 1816 there were counted, besides the church, the congregation-house, the two school and two choir-houses, thirty-six family houses in Salem, probably including those built in that year by A. Steiner, Foltz, and Hagen.

In the following years, not all the new buildings seem to have been recorded in the Memorabilia; hence the list is incomplete, but still not without local interest.

1817—1851.

1817. Senseman.
1819. Addition to the Sisters' house, on the south. John Vogler and Sam. Schulz.
1820. Thomas Wohlfahrt, Charles Levering, and Henry Herbst.
1821. New grist-mill near Salem.
1822. H. Lienbach, Schaffner, S. Lick, and Ackerman.
1823. A. Steiner, Jr. Cistern in the square.
1824. Philip Reich, Traug. Lienbach, Sam. Schulz.
1826. Three new houses.
1827. Two new houses. Printing-office.
1828. One new house.
1829. "   "   "
1831. L. Eberhardt, Denke, and Jos. Stauber.
1832. Timothy Vogler.
1834. Jos. Stauber.

APPENDIX.

1839. Clewell and Sussdorf.
1840. Wm. Houser, Theoph. Vierling, Chas. Cooper.
1841. Kramer, F. Fries, Beitel, A. Fishel, second story on Jac. Blum's store, chapel, minister's house for Bishop Van Vleck, corpse-house.
1842. Theod. Schultz, H. Meinung, A. Steiner, H. Winkler, John Chitty, Traug. Chitty.
1843. David Blum.
1844. Joshua Boner, J. D. Siewers, F. C. Meinung; concert hall.
1847. Edwin Beitel; bank building.
1848. Edwin Meinung; Fries, factory building.
1849. Antoinette Blum, Ed. Belo; hall of Young Men's Missionary Society and Sons of Temperance—the former in 1856 occupied by the post-office.
1851. Wm. F. Schulz.

No. IV.
ADDITIONS AND NOTES.

1753. The following are the names of the nine Brethren, who arrived as first settlers:—

John Beroth, farmer, from the Susquehanna, Pa.
John Lisher, farmer.
Herman Lœsh, miller, from Pennsylvania.
Jacob Lung, gardener, from Wurtemberg.
Christopher Merkle, baker.
Erich Ingebresten, carpenter, from Norway.
Henry Feldhausen, carpenter and hunter.
Hans Peterson, tailor from Denmark.
Jacob Pfeil, shoemaker, from Wurtemberg.

1757. Among those coming to the Bethabara mill, are mentioned Mr. Shephard and Mr. Banner.

1760. Two hives of bees were brought from Tar River, 120 miles, which increased very fast; in consequence, many bears made their appearance in the fall.

In December, immense quantities of wild pigeons made their appearance and roosted near by for nearly a month. When together, at night, they covered only a small tract of woods, but were clustered so thick upon the trees as to break down the largest limbs by their weight. The noise made by them in coming to their camp at night, as well as the fluttering, &c.

during the night, and thus breaking up in the morning, was heard at a considerable distance. The spot was marked for many years.

1761. Jan. very cold, and thick ice on the mill-pond, strong enough to drag heavy logs over it to the saw-mill.

1763. In Bethabara and Bethania wells were dug, and the first pumps introduced into this part of the country.

1765. John Leinbach, with his family of seven children, arrived from Oley, Pa., and bought lot No. 1, the so-called "Lineback tract."

1767. The County Court in Salisbury gave permits for three public roads, one leading from Salem to the Townfork and Dan River, another to Belo's Creek and the Cape Fear Road, and the third southward to the Uwharee.

1769. Great abundance of wild grapes; nineteen hogsheads of wine were made in the three settlements.

1770. Abundance of caterpillars, which destroyed much of the grass and grain. The place for the burial-ground of Salem was cleared and fenced in. Roads opened to Salisbury and Cross Creek.

1771. Much harm done to the corn by the squirrels, also many bears in the woods.

1772. A bell of 2758 lbs. weight arrived from Pennsylvania; the largest in the neighborhood; was used in Salem for meetings, and also served for the town-clock, to announce the hours.

In Oct., Br. Beelitscher finished an organ of two stops for Salem. Trombones had been procured from Europe in 1765.

A road was laid out from Salem to the Shallow Ford, which opened communication with Douthid's settlement; an old road to Belo's Creek was re-opened.

1778. Dobb's Parish abolished by law; no distinction of religious denominations henceforth. Salem waterworks; erected by J. Krause.

1780. Coffee three shillings per pound; sugar four shillings.

1781. First inoculation of smallpox in Salem.

1784. One hundred and one persons in Salem had the measles, only one child died; very hot summer; severe freshets; many sick of fever and sore throats.

1785. Fire-engines for Salem brought from Europe.

1786. While digging the cellar for addition to the Brethrens' house, Br. A. Kremser was covered and killed by the falling ground.

1787. Introduction of lightning-rods in Salem.

1789. In Bethabara, English preaching every fourth Sunday.

APPENDIX.

1791. Paper-mill near Salem finished; town clock in Salem.
1792. Fourteen persons died in Salem in February and March of an epidemic scarlet rash.
> The mail from Halifax to Salisbury passes through Salem once in two weeks; G. Shober, postmaster.
>
> A double row of sycamores was planted from the tavern to the bridge on the beach; still noble trees.

1795. Great freshet; the lower part of the mill under water. Wheat cost six shillings, corn four shillings—double price.
1796. Great freshet in January. Will. Hall, whilst riding to the mill, was drowned.
1797. Preaching places at the Muddy Creek, ten miles, and at Beaver Dam, thirteen miles from Salem.
1799. Br. Van Zevely worked a year with Br. Bachman, of Litiz, at the organ of the Salem church, building the outer organ case.
1802. Eighty persons in Salem inoculated with the cowpox.
1803. One hundred and twenty-five persons in Salem sick of the measles.
1806. The town-clock improved by Eberhard to strike the quarters.

Charles F. Bagge built a storehouse on the road to Friedland, the first house in *Charlestown* or *Waughtown*.

1811. March. Consecration of Rippel's church; cupola and bell on Bethabara church.

1814. One hundred and twenty persons in Salem sick with the measles.

1815. Mill on the Brushy Fork.
Wool-carding machinery of Br. Zevely, the first in this State.

1817. Great abundance of peaches and apples.

1828. Improvements in the water-works of Salem.

1831. By legislative enactment, the freedom from military service rescinded, which was formerly granted to the Moravians.
July 4th. Salem volunteer company.

1832. New fire engine from Philadelphia.

1833. Aug. 28th. Very destructive hail-storm; about four thousand window-panes broken.

1837. Salem cotton factory commenced operations in fall.

1840. Woollen factory of F. Fries.

1846. Union meetings in Liberty or Burchrentown.

1849. Emigration to Iowa.
Fifty-one acres of Salem land sold to the county of Forsythe, for $5 per acre, for the new county-town of *Winston*.

1850. Aug. 25th. Great freshet; bridge over the Middle Fork destroyed.
Court-house in Winston finished.

1854. Plank-road from Fayetteville to Bethania; church in Salem repaired; third gallery for boarders of academy.

1857. Jan. 18th. Severe snow-storm and intense cold; no mail from the North for nearly two weeks. Separation of town and church officers in Salem, and election of the first municipal officers, January 5th.

At the commencement of the year 1857, the governing Boards in the various departments (both Church and State) in Salem were composed as follows:—

Rev. L. T. Reichel, Pres't, }
Rev. G. F. Bahnson, } Provincial Board.
E. A. de Schweinitz, }

Rev. G. F. Bahnson, Minister at Salem.
S. Th. Pfohl, Warden of Congregation.
E. A. de Schweinitz, Administrator of Land-Office.
Rev. R. de Schweinitz, Principal of Salem Female Academy.

Rev. L. T. Reichel, }
Rev. G. F. Bahnson, } Trustees of Salem Female Academy.
E. A. de Schweinitz, }

E. A. de Schweinitz, Pres't,
S. Th. Pfohl, Secretary,
H. Leinbach,
Fr. Fries,
E. A. Vogler,
C. Cooper,
T. F. Keehln,
N. Vogler,
W. Petersen,
} Board of Overseers of the Congregation and Church Property.

Rev. G. F. Bahnson, President of Salem Boys' School.

S. Th. Pfohl,
Fr. Fries,
E. A. Vogler,
L. Belo,
} Committee of Salem Boys' School.

Charles Brietz, Mayor.

R. L. Patterson,
F. Fries,
A. Butner,
J. R. Crist,
E. Belo,
T. F. Keehln,
S. Mickey,
} Town Commissioners.

THE END.

www.ingramcontent.com/pod-product-compliance
Lightning Source LLC
Chambersburg PA
CBHW051054160426
43193CB00010B/1180